ARCHITECTS of ADJUSTMENT

Kennikat Press
National University Publications
Series in American Studies

ARCHITECTS
of
ADJUSTMENT

The History of the Psychological Profession in the United States

DONALD S. NAPOLI

National University Publications
KENNIKAT PRESS // 1981
Port Washington, N.Y. // London

Manufactured in the United States of America

Published by
Kennikat Press Corp.
Port Washington, N.Y. / London

Library of Congress Cataloging in Publication Data

Napoli, Donald S 1941-
    Architects of adjustment.

    (Series in American studies) (National university
publications)
    Bibliography: p.
    Includes index.
    1. Psychology—United States—History.
2. Psychology, Applied—United States—History.
I. Title.
BF108.U5N36   158'.9'0973   80-18990
ISBN 0-8046-9269-6

For my family

CONTENTS

ACKNOWLEDGMENTS

Of the many people who aided in gathering materials for this study, I would like especially to thank: Andrew W. Montgomery, for showing me such hospitality during my stay in Washington; John A. Popplestone and Marion White McPherson, for facilitating my use of the archives in Akron; Daniel Harris, for furnishing copies of documents relating to the Psychologists League and for discussing the league's operations with me; Kerry W. Buckley, Lorenz J. Finison, Nathan G. Hale, Jr., David Krech, Franz Samelson, and Michael J. Sokal, for sharing their unpublished research with me; and the Interlibrary Loan Department of the Shields Library at the University of California, Davis, for ferreting out countless obscure books and periodicals. My appreciation also goes to the many psychologists who took the time to answer my questions about their professional experiences.

Several people read and commented on the drafts of one or more chapters. I would like to thank Marvin Brienes, Linda Fritschner, Rebecca Greene, Nathan Hale, Daniel Harris, Conner Sorensen, and Mary Grace Taylor for their advice and interest. Special appreciation goes to Morgan B. Sherwood, Donald C. Swain, and particularly C. Roland Marchand, for their thorough reading of the original manuscript, and to Lorenz Finison for his many helpful suggestions on the revision.

ARCHITECTS of ADJUSTMENT

ABBREVIATIONS

AAAP	American Association for Applied Psychology
ACP	Association of Consulting Psychologists
AHAP	Archives of the History of American Psychology, University of Akron, Akron, Ohio
APA	American Psychological Association
APA Coll.	American Psychological Association Collection, Library of Congress, Washington, D.C.
CAA	Civil Aeronautics Authority
JCP	*Journal of Consulting Psychology*
NCWP	National Council of Women Psychologists
NRC	National Research Council
OPP	Office of Psychological Personnel
OSRD	Office of Scientific Research and Development
SPSSI	Society for the Psychological Study of Social Issues
WPA	Works Progress Administration

ABOUT THE AUTHOR

Donald S. Napoli is a historian at the California Office of Historic Preservation in Sacramento. He received his Ph.D. in history from the University of California at Davis, where he specialized in social history. He is the author of "The Mobilization of American Psychologists, 1938-1941" in *Military Affairs.*

INTRODUCTION

"Tired of the dating game?" asked a San Francisco newspaper advertisement in May 1974. A local business firm, Datamate, had the solution. For qualified applicants it guaranteed to find compatible members of the opposite sex, and it invited readers to "meet thoroughly screened people chosen for you after your personal evaluation by licensed psychologists."[1] The company offered more than match-ups by computer; it promised to apply psychology, the study of human mind and behavior, to the problems of its clients. It pledged further that the work would be done not by ordinary employees but by professionals of certified competence.

This intervention in American courtship provides but one instance of psychologists in action. During 1975 the press reported many others. There was, for example, "assertiveness training," a new technique for helping people stand up for their rights. *Newsweek* gave credit to two psychologists for popularizing this approach, which it called "the latest panacea of the human-potential movement." Meanwhile "behavior modification," another psychological technique used on a wide range of problems, was also winning many new adherents. In an Associated Press dispatch the director of the National Institute of Mental Health estimated that as many as fifty thousand Americans were undergoing this type of therapy in the summer of 1975. On a more modest scale, *Writer's Digest* reported good news for authors unaccountably stymied in their work: a New York psychologist had recently cured two severe cases of "writer's block."[2]

Psychologists were also providing services to business and industry. In New York City a number of firms sent employees to an all-day workshop directed by a psychologist and devoted to transactional analysis.

3

This psychological technique, observed *Nation's Business*, was "being employed by some corporations to help personnel at all levels use their mental capabilities for problem-solving and decision-making." Meanwhile a team of industrial psychologists was perfecting a test that uncovered accident proneness by measuring momentary inattention. An article in *Psychology Today* explained that businesses could use the test to insure that accident-prone workers were not placed in jobs where lapses of attention might prove dangerous.[3]

Other psychological tests made the news. In Pennsylvania civil libertarians complained about an attitude questionnaire given to each public school student; they requested that a panel of psychologists be brought in to determine the validity of the test. In Washington a five-year-old black child failed a psychological test that purportedly measured readiness for kindergarten; his parents charged that the test was racially biased. And in California a court appointed a clinical psychologist as one of the experts who would determine the mental competence of the recently arrested newspaper heiress Patricia Hearst.

Psychologists were, in short, providing a variety of services in a wide range of settings. By reporting only what was newsworthy, however, the press necessarily painted a distorted and incomplete picture of psychology's role in American society. Readers may have received the impression that ordinary people who behaved normally and felt reasonably contented could live their lives unaffected by applied psychology. Although undoubtedly there was something strange and faddish about much of what psychologists did, they had long argued that everyone needed their services, and as the twentieth century progressed an increasing number of people agreed with them. By 1975 applied psychology influenced the lives of virtually all Americans.

While psychology had its most direct effect on the many thousands who underwent psychological counseling, it also touched the lives of countless others through the omnipresent psychological test. Most Americans began having their psyches measured as soon as they learned to read. For the next twenty or thirty years they took tests of intelligence, aptitudes, and even more nebulous characteristics. By the time their own round of testing was completed (usually whey they settled into permanent jobs), they were beginning to worry about the test scores of their children. Managers of various institutions became increasingly fond of psychological tests. School administrators used I.Q. scores to establish "tracking" systems; colleges admitted students partly on the basis of the results of "scholastic aptitude" tests; professional and graduate schools predicted the success of applicants with the help of psychological examinations; and employers used tests of "vocational aptitude" and other mental qualities to select and promote workers. Thus, applied psychologists, either directly or through their tests, affected nearly everyone in the country. As a result, how and why they managed to achieve such influence have become important historical questions.

In part the growth of applied psychology can be explained by changes in American society during the twentieth century. Many institutions—businesses, schools, government—became larger and more complex. To an increasing extent they developed hierarchical organizations in which bureaucratic procedures minimized the discretion of individual employees. Work became more specialized and often more esoteric. Through centralized direction and planning these institutions attempted to make the most efficient use of available resources. By promising to bring the personalities of their workers and clients within the realm of human understanding and control, applied psychology offered managers an important tool in further rationalizing their operations. American institutions could make good use of psychological services, and applied psychologists had only to find a way to mobilize this need in their own behalf.

Changes in American society affected individuals as well. As never before, the nation became a land of opportunity: people took increasing control over what career they would pursue, whom they would marry, how they would spend their incomes—even what they would believe. As choices proliferated, the making of decisions became increasingly difficult. Meanwhile human relationships assumed a more transient and superficial quality, and people found less occasion to express their thoughts and feelings before receptive audiences. Life became more puzzling and more frustrating; it taxed the inner resources of each person. Psychology offered the same kind of service to individuals that it did to institutions: it promised to explore the psyche rationally and scientifically with the aim of providing each person greater understanding and control of his own personality. Again modern society generated a need for psychological services that applied psychologists could move to fill.

Another characteristic of twentieth-century America was the growth of applied science. Americans increasingly sought experts with scientific credentials to solve individual and social problems. Hybrid crops, new metal alloys, inorganic fertilizers, computers, television, the birth control pill—the list of technical innovations and refinements seemed to grow almost daily. Applied psychologists could turn this confidence in science to their own advantage. Their opportunities would depend in large measure on the extent to which they could get themselves accepted as true scientists.

The rise of the applied psychologists was related to one other aspect of the modernizing of America—the professionalization of work. With increasing job specialization came greater reliance on technical competence. While most jobs became more routine, some grew so complex that they were largely incomprehensible to outsiders. Managers and clients found themselves trying to supervise employees whose skills they could not duplicate or perhaps even judge. Workers in many occupations meanwhile banded together. Those who thought that their jobs required a diminishing amount of skill and judgment formed labor unions. Others who believed that they possessed and used special knowledge and abilities formed professional organizations. Both groups attempted to gain greater control over their work. The "professionals" sought higher social status as well. They hoped to win a public acknowledgment that their skills went far beyond those employed by clerical and blue collar workers.

Many groups of workers, especially those dealing directly with the public, began referring to themselves as professionals. Americans found themselves transacting business with "professional" hairdressers, travel agents, automobile mechanics, and the like. Most of this professionalism was merely self-attributed, and the public generally remained unimpressed. For groups like doctors and lawyers, however, professionalism was clearly something more. These groups enjoyed great success in establishing practices high in public esteem and free from outside interference. They thus staked the strongest claim to professionalism, although not even their work became universally admired or completely autonomous. Like other nonunion groups applied psychologists sought professional status. The growth of applied psychology thus became intimately connected with the psychologists' efforts to establish themselves as true professionals.

The academic study of professions has fallen mainly to the sociologists. They have been less intrigued by the element of status seeking in professionalization than by the characteristics that define a model profession. Sociologists have expended much effort in trying to establish criteria by which they could judge the degree of professionalism in various occupational groups. One early study found three essential features of a profession: the performance of a service to others, the application of "specialized intellectual study and training," and the regular payment of its members by fee or salary. Another list added these characteristics: the recognition by the client of the professional's authority, the sanction of the community (through, for example, licensing and the accreditation of training schools), the presence of an ethical code for members, and the existence of a "professional culture." There are many other such lists. Although each is slightly different from the rest, together they provide a fairly clear general conception of professionalism.[4]

In seeking precision and universality, however, professional "models" necessarily become static and ahistorical. A less rigorous definition will perhaps turn out to be more useful in a historical study: thus, a profession may be defined as an occupational group that enjoys high prestige among clients, employers, the general public, and the practitioners in other prestigious fields. Professionalization may then be considered as the series of activities that members of occupational groups undertake in order to achieve professional status. Particular attributes become important only insofar as aspiring professionals believe them to be characteristic of genuine professions and try to institute them in their own group. Furthermore, prestige, an admittedly nebulous quality, does have an empirical dimension, since periodic opinion polls have ranked the public esteem of occupations since 1925. Not coincidentally, the occupations with the highest ratings—medicine, for example—were the ones that sociologists used to abstract the essential characteristics of a profession and thus build their professional models.

Defining professionalization as the quest for high social status works well in the case of the applied psychologists. Specific circumstances may have made them unusually desirous of a good reputation. They received their training from college professors, who already enjoyed high public repute, and they often worked with psychiatrists, whose association with medicine conferred high esteem. Their close link to members of highly prestigious occupations may thus have kept them especially aware of their own status. This characteristic of psychologists may apply less readily to other groups, however. So the search for the essential qualities of a profession has not ended and could probably continue indefinitely. Students can easily agree with one sociologist who recently suggested that "perhaps a historical approach to the development of occupations is the best antidote for the attribute rut."[5]

Most histories of professions have been written by the professionals themselves. These works usually focus on the development of current practice and thus fail to provide a broad understanding of the profession's past. Many are merely chronologies filled with anecdotes and undigested information. In 1965 the historian Oscar Handlin lamented that "practically nothing is known about the history of the professions in the United States." Handlin called for studies that "rested directly on primary sources" and would "throw light upon the evolution of the organized structure" of the various professions.[6]

Scholars have heeded Handlin's call. Daniel H. Calhoun had already made a start in that direction with his book *The American Civil Engineer* (1960). Other works have followed. In recent years doctors, lawyers, librarians, teachers, social workers, and foreign service officers have all received full-length treatment. The development of professions has thus become an accepted and growing subject for historical inquiry.

The experience of applied psychology differed from that of other professions in several important respects. First, the professionalization of psychology can be related not merely to general social trends such as bureaucratization but to specific events as well. Between 1920 and 1945 applied psychologists found themselves confronted with the after-shocks of World War 1, the economic crisis of the Great Depression, and the expanding opportunities of World War 2. To a large degree these events channeled the quest for professional status. They set the stage for the organizational struggles and intergroup rivalries experienced by applied psychologists during the period.

Second, the professionalization of applied psychology between 1920 and 1945 had little to do with scientific discoveries or technological innovations. The psychological test was invented in the nineteenth century, and nothing of comparable importance appeared afterward. Applied psychologists thus spent little time arguing with one another over the most effective techniques. They kept internecine warfare to a minimum and were able to present a united front against practitioners who lacked the requisite scientific training. Even the long and sometimes bitter struggle with psychiatrists did not rest on differences in technique. It was more a jurisdictional dispute, with applied psychologists claiming treatment rights over all people who were not demonstrably ill.

Finally, the applied psychologists were the first occupational group to start the journey to professionalism directly from the university. They recognized no nineteenth-century progenitors and thus never experienced the shift from volunteer work or apprenticeships to formal training. From the very beginnings of applied psychology the practitioners held college degrees. This situation provoked conflict with academic psychologists, who based their claim to professional status on their role as college professors. The academicians controlled psychological associations, journals, and graduate programs. They outnumbered the practitioners until the end of World War 2, and they were reluctant to endanger their prestige as scholars and scientists by promoting the desires of their nonacademic colleagues.

Until recently applied psychologists could claim to be the only occupational group with academic origins. Economists always provided something of an exception, although they took little interest in licensing, ethical codes, and the other trappings of professionalism. The economic slump of the 1970s, however, turned other disciplines toward applied fields in an attempt to place recent graduates and bolster sagging enrollments. In 1975, for example, the American Association of Geographers began to seek ways to make graduate work in geography more practical. Sociologists also hoped to expand their nonacademic job opportunities by finding more work in "applied sociology." Even historians started to think along these lines. A session at a branch meeting of the American Historical Association in 1975 was devoted to discussing new jobs in "applied history." Questions arose about winning the confidence of the public, insuring the objectivity of applied historians, and maintaining the scholarly excellence of graduate education. They were the questions that psychology had been facing for over a half-century, and they gave further indication that other disciplines might begin taking the road to professionalism that psychologists had traversed between 1920 and 1945.

An account of this journey may be a bit disorienting to observers of the current scene in psychology. For instance, the term "applied psychology" is not widely used today, nor are its three historical divisions —industrial, educational, and clinical—usually considered varieties of essentially the same activity. Similarly, the sixty-year conflict between the two working branches of psychology (the academicians and the practitioners) continues to blaze as hot as ever, but psychologists today often see it as a struggle between ideologies (behaviorist and Freudian) rather than occupations. Observers of the psychological profession must set aside some of their contemporary perceptions in order to view its history clearly.

The present study opens with a brief sketch of applied psychology from 1890 to 1920. During this period psychology emerged as a scientific discipline within the universities, and the American Psychological Association arose to serve the scholarly interests of psychologists. The three main fields of psychological application—industrial, educational, and clinical—had their beginnings, and the First World War accelerated the development of each.

Chapter two takes a short detour from the chronological account of applied psychology to examine the concept of adjustment. Upon this notion applied psychologists laid their claim to be trustworthy scientists with an important service to perform. Adjustment also provided the key to their social thought and their hopes for a better world.

The next two chapters trace the quest for professional status through the 1920s and 1930s. In these years applied psychologists saw the public's enthusiasm for their services replaced by caution and often disillusionment. They came to realize that they must organize if they were to overcome their foes and win public confidence. Since they lacked the wherewithal to move effectively on their own, the attitude of their academic colleagues became the crucial element in these organizational efforts.

The Second World War proved to be the major turning point for applied psychology. Chapter five examines the psychologists' work in the war itself, detailing their widespread acceptance and their most important accomplishments. Chapter six focuses on wartime organizational changes, which under a temporary cloak of unity put the resources of the American Psychological Association at the disposal of applied psychologists. By 1945 applied psychologists had won public confidence and had organized themselves to fill the burgeoning demand for their services. They were unalterably on the road to professional status.

Chapter seven outlines events of the postwar period. In these years applied psychology enjoyed unwavering popular interest, and practitioners experienced an unprecedented prosperity. They easily won the battles for certification, ethical codes, and similar badges of professionalism. The expansion of applied psychology, however, brought diversity, and with it came a splintering unknown in the years between 1920 and 1945. The future thus promised some additional problems in the search for professionalism.

The conclusion briefly reviews the main themes of the book: the applied psychologists' repeated efforts to establish an effective professional organization; the threats to applied psychology posed by charlatans, psychiatrists, and academicians; the varying public demand for expert assistance in adjustment; and the effects of World War 2 in accelerating the applied psychologists' drive for professional status.

1

THE BEGINNINGS OF APPLIED PSYCHOLOGY

"The measurements and statistics of psychology, which, at first sight, may seem remote from common interests, may in the end become the most important factor in the progress of society."[1] With these brave words one of America's leading psychologists, James McKeen Cattell, concluded a statement on the value of his science in medicine, art, and politics. He was not reviewing decades of accomplishment but instead voicing a hope for the distant future. Cattell spoke in 1893, barely fifteen years after the beginning of experimental psychology and before any of its applications were making an impact on society. It was an optimistic prediction made in a time of great opportunities.

The formative years of applied psychology—the period between 1890 and 1920—witnessed vast changes in American society. In the same year that Cattell made his bright forecast for the future of psychology, the historian Frederick Jackson Turner argued that the disappearance of an identifiable frontier in 1890 marked the end of "the first period of American history."[2] Almost two decades later Turner detailed the characteristics of the new era: an "upleaping wealth and organization and concentration of industrial power," "the monopoly of the fundamental industrial processes by huge aggregations of capital," an "unprecedented immigration to supply the centers of industrial life," "the massing of population in the cities and the contemporaneous increase of urban power," the disappearance of "the old pioneer individualism" in favor of "the forces of social combination," a growing conflict between unrestricted liberty and popular government leading to "an extraordinary federal activity in limiting individual and corporate freedom for the benefit of society," and finally a new involvement in international affairs

11

including "dependencies and protectorates" abroad.[3] Applied psychology emerged during a turbulent era, and its early development benefited from the social changes that Turner catalogued.

The transformation of American society started before 1890, of course, and the settlement of the West continued afterward. The disappearance of the frontier merely symbolized the waning of the old order and the rise of new problems and challenges. Coincidentally, 1890 also marked the beginning of applied psychology, for in that year Cattell published the results of the first psychological testing program. The tests were perhaps a symbol of the new order, in which Americans, having conquered the natural environment, moved to bring the mind within their control as well. If the old frontier was closing, a new one was opening up. In a sense, the applied psychologists were the first permanent settlers on this new frontier.

Philosophers had speculated about the mind for centuries, but scientific psychology emerged only toward the close of the nineteenth century. It took root first in Germany, where Wilhelm Wundt established a laboratory at the University of Leipzig in 1879. Wundt, trained in medicine and formerly an instructor of physiology, soon became recognized as the leader of the new field. Students from many countries, including the United States, came to Leipzig to learn about his system, which became known as structuralism. Its method was introspection, in which a trained subject reported on his consciousness during various phases of an experiment. Wundt hoped to isolate the elements of consciousness, discover how they were connected to one another, and thus determine the structure of the mind.

Wundt was seeking general laws, and he was uninterested in the differences that occurred in the observations of his subjects. Cattell, however, who received his doctorate from Leipzig in 1886, considered the individual to be the crucial variable in the experiments. His studies of individual differences, which were strongly influenced by the work of Sir Francis Galton in England, continued after his return to the United States, and their focus helped significantly in the development of applied psychology. In 1890 Cattell coined the term "mental test" in an article in which he described his work with students at the University of Pennsylvania. His tests measured color vision, sensitivity to pain, reaction time, keenness of hearing, rote memory, and similar qualities. He gathered the data not in order to learn something about the mind in general but rather to establish statistical uniformities among those tested. He also aimed for something in addition to psychological truth: he wanted to find a means of selecting the college applicants who had the best chances for success.

Cattell's quest for practical results typified American science in the nineteenth century. His demand for quantified data marked the beginning of a still-powerful trend in American psychology—shared by academicians and practitioners alike—which held that characteristics of the psyche can and should be expressed in numerical terms.

On a theoretical level, meanwhile, a native American view of psychology arose to challenge structuralism. The main problem with Wundt and his followers, argued William James, was their supposition that consciousness remained stationary rather than moving in a continuous, changing stream. Thus, they looked for structure where none existed. Other psychologists expanded on James's belief in the purposive nature of the mind. They emphasized the constant interaction and mutual adaptation of the mind and the environment. This approach, called functionalism, was closely related to evolutionary theory and pragmatic philosophy. Psychology became in this view the study of an individual's adjustment to his surroundings, and applied psychology took as its goal the facilitating of that adjustment. By 1900 applied psychology in the United States already had a subject—individual differences—and a purpose—individual adjustment.

Applied psychology also required a staging area, and this was to be the university. The late nineteenth century witnessed the differentiation of the social sciences into new academic disciplines. From subjects like moral philosophy and political economy there arose not only psychology but also sociology, anthropology, economics, and political science. The particular problem of American psychologists was differentiating themselves from philosophers. The growth of graduate schools and the increasing specialization of study eased their efforts. Johns Hopkins offered the first doctoral program in psychology. G. Stanley Hall, a student of both James and Wundt, received a full-time appointment there in 1882, and the school produced America's first Ph.D. in psychology four years later. In 1889 Harvard changed William James's title from professor of philosophy to professor of psychology.

In the next fifteen years psychology made rapid advances in academe. By 1904 sixty-two colleges offered at least three psychology courses, and eight large universities required psychology for the bachelor of arts degree. Meanwhile American graduate schools had produced over one hundred Ph.D.s in psychology. In the period between 1898 and 1903, psychology ranked fourth—behind chemistry, zoology, and physics—in doctoral degrees granted in the sciences. The number of academic institutions with psychological laboratories also grew. In the twenty years after Hall founded the laboratory at Johns Hopkins in 1883, forty-seven others arose. Thus, by the turn of the century psychology held a secure place in academe, and the prospects for growth in that setting looked bright.

To communicate the results of their research and to promote a sense of identification with the new discipline, psychologists at the turn of the century founded a number of scholarly periodicals. Hall initiated the first such publication in the United States, the *American Journal of Psychology*, in 1887, and he quickly followed that with the *Pedagogical Seminary* in 1891. Two years later Cattell and James Mark Baldwin organized the Psychological Review Company, which launched two new journals, the *Psychological Review* (1894) and the *Psychological Bulletin* (1904); a series of lengthy studies, *Psychological Monographs* (1895); and an annual bibliography, the *Psychological Index* (1895). The list of periodicals continued to grow in the twentieth century.

Like specialists in other fields, psychologists sought to develop a national community of their peers. The formation of the American Psychological Association (APA) in 1892 provided an important step in this direction. Hall invited six of his colleagues—including James, Cattell, and Baldwin—to join him at the organizational meeting. These seven, convening in July, chose a president, a secretary-treasurer, and an executive committee and elected twenty-four others to membership. They then engaged in what was to become the main activity at subsequent meetings—listening to each other's research papers. In 1894 the APA adopted its first constitution, which defined its purpose as "the advancement of Psychology as a science" and limited its membership to those who were "engaged in this work."[4] A clarification of these terms began almost at once, and in a sense it has never ended.

The APA insisted that its membership be composed of psychologists of proven scholarship. In 1896 it required that the contributions to psychology of prospective members be posted at the annual meeting. The following year it developed an application blank with spaces for occupational position, publications, and the names of two sponsors already in the organization. These provisions excluded amateurs, but they did nothing to rid the association of those philosophical psychologists who preferred to speculate rather than experiment. In its early years the APA was happy to include such scholars; in fact, it elected John Dewey president in 1899 and Josiah Royce in 1901. But as early as 1895 one member proposed a special section of the association for philosophers, and the following year it was suggested that the philosophers form their own organization. In 1901 they did just that, withdrawing from the APA to form the American Philosophical Association. Their departure greatly increased the homogeneity of the APA and did not slow its growth for long. Membership rose steadily from 127 in 1900 to 393 in 1920.

The APA received the first challenge to its national hegemony in 1904. Edward Bradford Titchener of Cornell, a structuralist in the European tradition, objected to the personnel, policies, and perhaps the whole idea of the association. He wrote to sixteen American psychologists—including four ex-presidents of the APA—proposing a new organization to be called the American Society for the Advancement of Experimental Psychology. The responses proved discouraging; nine of the sixteen expressed serious reservations about undermining the APA. Titchener denied that he was forming a rival group, and it is doubtful that he had the temperament to lead a successful secession. What emerged was a series of small annual get-togethers during which psychologists invited by Titchener informally discussed their research. "The experimentalists," as the participants at these meetings came to be called, held high prestige among psychologists, but they never had the potential for becoming a broad-based national organization. (In the 1920s they were to re-form as the openly elitist Society of Experimental Psychologists.) The threat disappeared, and the APA solidified its position as the largest and most representative group of American psychologists. Its direction would be challenged in the future but never its preeminence.

During this early period when psychology was winning academic recognition and becoming nationally organized, some psychologists looked for ways to apply their study to practical problems. Testing continued, but the premise that the quality of the mind could be determined by measuring its supposedly elemental characteristics (reaction time, visual acuity, etc.) proved fruitless. Nevertheless, tests aroused popular interest, of which the APA took advantage in its first public relations venture in 1893. One of the association's founders set up a display at the Columbian Exposition in Chicago. Here for a small fee people could have their "sense capacities and mental powers" tested. The organizer of the display reported much public interest, but he was unable to turn the mounds of data he accumulated into something of practical value. As it happened, mental testing would begin to bloom in America only after the introduction of the Binet scale in 1908. Clinical and industrial psychology were to develop first.

In the spring of 1896 an elementary school principal approached the head of the psychological laboratory at the University of Pennsylvania, Lightner Witmer, with an educational problem. One of the students in her school showed a deficiency in spelling, and she wanted to know what psychology could do to diagnose and treat the condition. Witmer knew that while psychologists had not studied spelling problems per se, they had examined the memory, from which such problems might originate. He decided to try to help the child. "It appears to me," he later commented, "that if psychology was worth anything to me or others it should be able to assist the efforts of a teacher in a retarded case of this kind."[5] Witmer began to aid other children as well, spending several hours a week on their deficiencies. America's first psychological clinic was born.

Witmer, a former student of both Wundt and Cattell, had become the head of the laboratory at the University of Pennsylvania in 1891. His experiences in treating children's educational problems in 1896 made him a strong advocate of applying psychology in this way. At the APA meeting in December of that year, he outlined a grand plan for increasing the number of clinics and expanding their services to include cooperation with physicians and the training of new psychologists. It was Witmer who coined the terms "clinical psychology" and "psychological clinic." The clinical method, he explained, involved observation, experimentation, and "pedagogical treatment" of an individual with the purpose of altering and developing his mind. Witmer believed this method was applicable to adults as well as children.

Witmer expanded his work. He developed strong ties to the educational establishment in Philadelphia, and he considered the clinic a part of the movement for better compensatory education which developed around the turn of the century. He also worked closely with physicians and a variety of charities and social service agencies. In 1906 he founded the *Psychological Clinic,* a journal that published reports of clinical work. A year later Witmer supplemented his outpatient care with a hospital school that provided longer periods for observation and training. Children were admitted for a fee and might stay up to a year. His treatment of behavioral problems had a strong didactic streak and seemed usually to include doses of self-discipline and positive thinking.

Despite the effort Witmer put into it, he never devoted himself completely to the clinic. He was first of all a professor of psychology, and he continued to carry out his academic duties during the forty years he remained at the University of Pennsylvania. His career, in which an involvement in applied work was coupled with strong, permanent ties to academe, formed the pattern for many other leaders of applied psychology in America.

Psychologists at other universities began to follow Witmer's example. In 1908 the University of Minnesota established its Free Clinic in Mental Development. The clinic provided medical and psychological diagnosis and treatment of cases referred to it by the public schools, the juvenile court, and the Juvenile Protective League. Work in the clinic also formed the basis for a course on mental retardation given by the psychology department for prospective teachers. A year later a similar program arose in connection with a child welfare foundation at the University of Washington. The foundation operated two clinics that provided individual examinations and special classes for school children. It also worked with the juvenile court in Seattle, testing alleged delinquents before their hearings to determine if they were of sound mind. In 1913, for example, it examined 1,186 children for the court and discovered that 131 were functional neurotics, 111 mentally defective, 29 physically precocious, 7 morally deficient, and 2 psychotic. The number of these clinics began to grow more quickly. In 1914 American Institutions of higher learning were operating nineteen of them.

Psychological study and treatment of the mentally defective began as early as 1898, but the most notable work in this field started in 1905 when a research department was established at the Training School for the Feeble-Minded at Vineland, New Jersey. Henry H. Goddard, formerly one of Hall's students and soon to become America's foremost intelligence tester, was appointed director in 1906. Goddard set up the first laboratory in the country designed especially for clinical work. The operation expanded, and by 1912 it included a staff of nine who tested, observed, and treated the children and collected histories of their families. Goddard also deserves note as America's first permanent full-time psychologist who did not hold an academic appointment. His position thus provides a contrast with that of Witmer and others whose rank as college professors bestowed high public esteem.

In 1909 Grace Fernald set another important precedent: she became the first clinical psychologist to work under the supervision of a physician. In the clinics discussed so far the psychologists determined the appropriate treatment for their clients, but at the Chicago Juvenile Psychopathic Institute a neurologist, William Healy, clearly had command. He worked closely with Fernald and her successor, and he relied on them to administer tests to the youthful offenders, but he assumed ultimate responsibility for decisions made in the clinic. A similar situation developed in psychopathic hospitals. Beginning in 1904, a few psychologists worked in these institutions, but they were seldom allowed to treat patients. For the most part they carried out research more reminiscent of an academic laboratory than a psychological clinic. As in the case at Chicago, they did not define their own role. Thus began the unending confusion and conflict about psychologists' proper relationship to physicians.

Five years after Witmer founded his clinic, psychologists initiated their first sustained involvement in the problems of industry. In the fall of 1901 a Chicago advertising man approached Walter Dill Scott of Northwestern University to see if he would be interested in giving a talk explaining how psychology could be used in advertising. Scott had received his Ph.D.

with Wundt only a year before, and he had some doubts about getting involved in a subject so far removed from his laboratory. He finally agreed, but only after getting the approval of his superior colleague at Northwestern. When the advertisers met for dinner in December, Scott was there. "If we are able to find and . . . express the psychological laws upon which the art of advertising is based," he explained, "we shall have made a distinct advance, for we shall have added the science to the art of advertising."[6]

Scott's career soon became linked to business. One of the men at the meeting, the head of a large Chicago advertising firm, was so impressed with Scott's talk that he invited him to expand his ideas in a series of magazine articles. This venture began in 1902; in it Scott mixed psychological principles and practical advice. He also reported on a simple experiment done for the Burlington Railroad, which could not decide on a typeface for its timetables. Scott had subjects read schedules done in each style and determined the one that permitted greater speed and accuracy. In only a few years the psychology of advertising became sufficiently well established that Northwestern University designated Scott in 1909 professor of advertising as well as professor of psychology.

The manifesto of industrial psychology, Hugo Munsterberg's *Psychology and Industrial Efficiency,* appeared in 1912. Munsterberg had come to the United States from his native Germany to head the laboratory at Harvard, but like so many of Wundt's other students, he soon became involved in applications of the new science. In this book he saw psychology as an extension of the movement for "scientific management" that had been initiated by Frederick Taylor in the 1890s. Psychologists, he explained, could select the fittest person for each job and could set up working conditions that elicited the greatest productivity from employees. "The psychological experiment," he declared, "is systematically to be placed at the service of commerce and industry."[7] Munsterberg urged his colleagues to go forth from their laboratories and join him in this worthy enterprise.

A few psychologists took up the cause. They did most of their early work on selection tests, hoping to find a quick and simple method to determine if a job applicant had the required mental capacities for a given position. Munsterberg led the way with tests for motormen, telephone operators, ship's officers, and traveling salesmen. Other psychologists soon developed examinations for telegraphers, typists, and stenographers. In 1915 a Cleveland clothing manufacturer used the first tests for choosing industrial workers. Meanwhile Scott was working on other aids in selection: an application blank, a standardized letter to former employers, and forms to help an interviewer objectively judge the traits of an applicant and to aid in making comparisons between him and present employees. In 1915 the Carnegie Institute of Technology in Pittsburgh established a division of applied psychology under the direction of Walter Van Dyke Bingham. For Bingham, who had been teaching at Dartmouth, it marked the beginning of a long and influential career in industrial psychology. Almost as soon as he arrived in Pittsburgh, he met the owner of a large insurance agency, who suggested that the new division offer a course in salesmanship. Bingham had no objections in principle, but he believed more research was needed about what made a successful salesman. He thus proposed establishing a research bureau, funded by private businesses, to study this question. He borrowed Scott from Northwestern to head the new Bureau of Salesmanship Research and invented for him the title professor of applied psychology.

The movement to apply psychological methods to management problems made much progress between 1913 and 1917. Businessmen were beginning to believe that psychology actually could help to heighten efficiency and increase profits. The list of sponsors for the Bureau of Salesmanship Research revealed this widespread interest. Included were the Ford Motor Company, Goodrich Tire and Rubber, Westinghouse Electric, Heinz Foods, Prudential Insurance, and Carnegie Steel. Although psychologists were turning more attention to industrial issues, they acted as consultants or advisers rather than full-time employees. In this period none was ready to sever his ties to academe.

The one activity that bound together all applied psychologists was testing. They entered every environment—school, clinic, or business—armed with various kinds of mental tests. For almost twenty years after Cattell began examining college students in 1890, American psychologists employed tests designed to measure specific mental qualities (memory, color vision, etc.). Although aided by developments in mathematics, including work on correlation coefficients and factor analysis, they had no method to evaluate general intelligence. Meanwhile Alfred Binet had been working in France on just this question, and in 1905 he and an associate produced a new kind of test. It consisted of thirty tasks of increasing difficulty; the more of them a child could perform successfully, the greater his intelligence—defined as the ability to make sound judgments—was considered to be.

The strongest advocate of the new test in the United States was Henry Goddard. When Goddard read a report on the Binet scale in 1908, he had some initial doubt that it could help in his diagnosis of the feeble-minded. Nonetheless, he translated the test into English and started using it at Vineland. He was happily surprised at its apparent accuracy in evaluating children's intelligence, and in 1909 he made a favorable report on it before the American Association for the Study of the Feebleminded. The following year this organization accepted his recommendation that Binet scores be used to classify the mentally deficient into three categories: idiots, imbeciles, and morons (a word Goddard invented). This schema put the mental age of the latter group between eight and twelve years. In 1911 he used his own studies to revise the Binet scale. Meanwhile he helped to unite intelligence testing with the eugenics movement when he joined the committee on feeble-mindedness of the American Breeders' Association's Committee on Eugenics.

Goddard turned the Vineland summer school for teachers into a training center for Binet testing. Its graduates joined others throughout the country in an effort to determine a precise measurement of American intelligence. Inmates of reformatories were a prime target, and testers soon found a shocking degree of what they considered feeble-mindedness among this group. A survey at Ohio institutions was a case in point. At the Girls Industrial Home 59 percent of the inmates registered as feeble-minded; at the Boys Industrial School 46 percent were feeble-minded and 26 percent on the borderline. Similar studies in Illinois, California, and Massachusetts yielded similar results. In Albany, New York, a team of intrepid testers examined local prostitutes and discovered 54 percent were feeble-minded. Statistics like these seemed to show a clear link between criminality and mental defect.

Yet even more disturbing to the public was Goddard's study of hereditary degeneracy, *The Kallikak Family,* published in 1912. In the book Goddard discussed the family of one of the inmates at Vineland. Its two branches had been sired over a hundred years before by a man Goddard called Martin Kallikak. One line was by a purportedly feeble-minded girl Kallikak met in a tavern, the other by a normal woman he later married. The marriage produced respectable, upstanding citizens, but the earlier liaison resulted in six generations of alcoholics, prostitutes, and other social undesirables. The explanation, Goddard believed, could only be hereditary—mental defect passed from parent to child.

Another puzzle remained. Goddard contended that "a large proportion of those who are considered feeble-minded in this study are persons who would not be recognized as such by the untrained observer."[8] Goddard believed that only psychological testing could consistently distinguish the normal from the defective, and he thought that psychologists, by helping to weed out the mentally incompetent from the rest of American society, would contribute greatly to the solution of many social problems. Goddard obviously had plans not only for the feeble-minded but for the psychologists as well. He staked a strong claim to professional status for psychologists by arguing that they had exclusive competence to perform an important public service.

Foreign immigrants provided another likely target for the testers. In 1911 one psychologist proposed that all suspected defectives be given a mental test and be prohibited from entering the country if found to be feeble-minded. A year later two members of the Vineland staff went to Ellis Island to see if they could determine how many mental defectives were among the newcomers. But for the most part psychologists had to wait until World War 1 before they could carry out these tests—and incidentally make a contribution to the debate about the intellectual capacities of different races and ethnic groups.

Testing enjoyed some popularity in the public schools. Educators found that a 1916 version of the Binet scale (dubbed the Stanford-Binet after the home base of its inventor, Lewis M. Terman) was especially useful because the score it produced did not necessarily increase as the child grew older. In this scheme mental age was divided by chronological age and multiplied by 100 to obtain an "intelligence quotient." Psychologists also worked on standardized tests in various subjects. Led by Edward L. Thorndike of Columbia, they produced examinations for arithmetic, handwriting, drawing, English composition, spelling, and reading. By 1918 educational researchers had developed well over one hundred such tests for different subjects and grades. These kinds of tests were still controversial, however. On the eve of American entry into the First World War, the struggle for "objective" achievement tests was not yet won, and the use of the I.Q. was still limited.

One aspect of the growing use of intelligence tests bothered psychologists. Many of the testers had little training in psychology, and because they had no basic understanding of what they were doing the results they obtained were questionable. As early as 1911 psychologists began discussing the possibility of developing standards to differentiate themselves from the testers. In 1915 the APA passed a resolution on the issue. Because psychological diagnosis required broad training and education in psychology, it declared, and because some people without this background were being engaged in this activity, "this Association discourages the use of mental tests for practical psychological diagnosis by individuals psychologically unqualified for this work."[9] Thus the APA made the first of its sporadic efforts to regulate psychological practice.

The association in 1915, however, was poorly equipped to combat unqualified practitioners. In the ten years previous it had (among other things) continued to raise its membership standards so that many Binet testers who might have been able to join the APA in 1905 were no longer eligible. In 1906 the association reinterpreted the membership requirement to bar those without full-time positions in psychology unless they had published acceptable psychological research. In 1911 it required applicants to enclose copies of their publications. Four years later it excluded people in academe who did not hold professorial rank. The 1915 resolution accomplished nothing. The association did not maintain any power over its members and had very little influence on public opinion. It could not hope to affect the activities of people like the testers who were not even allowed to join the organization. The twin issues—poorly trained practitioners and the APA's proper role in opposing them—remained unresolved. They would not come to a head until after the United States had entered World War 1.

Psychologists showed much interest in joining the war effort. On 6 April 1917, only two days after Congress declared war, a discussion of how psychology might become involved in national defense occurred at the annual meeting of Titchener's group of experimentalists. Robert M. Yerkes, who had worked on intelligence testing and who was currently president of the APA, presided over the session, which discussed a wide range of possible uses for psychology in the war. Even before this, however, some psychologists had been trying to stimulate government interest in their science, first through the American Association for the Advancement of Science (which the APA had joined in 1902) and then through the National Research Council. The coming of the war served to intensify this effort. Yerkes was quick to mobilize the APA, and he called a special meeting of its executive council for the end of April.

At the council meeting Yerkes set up twelve committees to deal with various aspects of psychology's service in the war. Few of them were to accomplish much, either because the chairmen refused to push the committee's skills upon the military or because the assigned tasks fell outside the realm of the psychologists' competence. The group established to study methods of selecting fliers was something of a special case, however. The Army Signal Corps, which had charge of aviation during the war, quickly accepted it and continued to support its work even though it produced few tangible results. The psychologists' main effort came through two committees: one, headed by Yerkes, focused on the psychological examination of new recruits; the other, eventually directed by Scott, dealt with selecting men for military jobs.

These were the two general fields of applied psychology that had received the most attention in the period before the war. Psychologists hoped that their work on intelligence testing and vocational selection in civilian life could be applied quickly and easily to military problems. They knew that the war presented them with a great opportunity to show what they could do. "Our knowledge and our methods are of importance to the military service of our country," Yerkes told his colleagues, "and it is our duty to cooperate to the fullest extent and immediately toward the increased efficiency of our Army and Navy."[10] But they also realized that the science and practice of psychology would suffer a heavy blow if they could not live up to their promises. "I am very jealous of the public reputation of psychologists," wrote a former president of the APA, "and I am extremely anxious that no committee of the Association enjoying either actual or nominal authority shall expose itself to ridicule or justify serious criticism."[11] The psychologists thus played their two best cards and hoped to be able to stay in the game.

For the first few months of the war, the work of what became Scott's committee amounted only to the efforts of Scott himself. Annoyed that the APA leadership was giving so much attention to intelligence testing, he set off on a one-man campaign to show that his rating scale, a form he had developed at Carnegie Institute of Technology, would be psychology's most important contribution to the war effort. Securing permission of the army, he made a tour of training camps during which he successfully demonstrated the device. In August army officials were sufficiently impressed by Scott's arguments and activities that they established the Committee on Classification of Personnel within the Adjutant General's Office.

Scott quickly helped to organize the committee, which besides himself included Yerkes, Bingham, Terman, Thorndike, Raymond Dodge of Wesleyan, and J. F. Shepard of the University of Michigan. Scott then recruited a group of businessmen to act as employment managers at army cantonments, received the first of a series of appropriations, and got down to work. As it turned out, the introduction of the rating scale became an insignificant part of the committee's duties. For the army had entered the war with virtually no plan for determining the occupational skills of its recruits and placing men in the most appropriate jobs. Nor, in fact, did it know how many or what type of skilled soldiers it needed to keep each of its units functioning. Army officials came to realize that this lack of information was a serious problem in an organization of 4 million men. "We can never expect to get maximum service out of any Army," declared the adjutant general in September 1917, "unless we have each man placed where he can serve best."[12] That became the job of Scott's committee.

Given the size and importance of its responsibilities, the committee was able to expand its operations quickly and with little opposition. The committee itself grew from an initial 20 to over 175; in addition, it oversaw the activities of some 7,500 men in personnel units that were springing up at army posts throughout the country. By the end of the war these units had interviewed and classified nearly 3,500,000 men, over a third of whom went on to specialized duties. The committee also established a trade tests division that developed proficiency examinations in various occupational specialities. This work began slowly, but by November 1918 it had yielded 112 tests for 83 military jobs. All in all, Scott's committee performed important work, enhancing the war effort and raising hopes for peacetime applications. It enjoyed much greater acceptance and accomplishment than the group assigned to measure the intelligence of recruits.

Yerkes's committee hoped originally to devise a test that would assess personality characteristics as well as mental capacity, but opposition within the military and a clear lack of experience with personality tests left intelligence as the focus of attention. Committee members realized meanwhile that the Binet scale, which had to be administered to people individually, would be too slow and cumbersome to use on all the thousands of army recruits.

The committee decided therefore to develop a standardized test that could be given to large numbers of men at once. Army officials approved a trial of the test in August 1917, and Yerkes, commissioned a major in the Sanitary Corps, began supervision of the army's testing program. After months of further refinement Yerkes and his coworkers published the Army Alpha Test in April 1918. It had questions about synonyms, numerical progressions, word relationships, and general knowledge. The Alpha was, in short, the progenitor of the intelligence tests that Americans would take by the tens of millions in the following decades.

The committee accomplished its task in the face of opposition from two sources. First, military psychiatrists saw intelligence testing as part of their own duty to eliminate the mentally unfit from the army, and they objected to independent activity by psychologists in this sphere. In May 1917 Yerkes grimly reported that the psychiatrists "desire to control the situation and to subordinate everything psychological to their will."[13] He felt compelled to deny that psychologists were trying to usurp the authority of psychiatrists, and he began to speak of the intelligence test as a means of classifying all recruits rather than weeding out the slow-witted. After a trial program was approved, the psychologists worked only under the control of medical officers. Commissions came in the Sanitary Corps, the unit within the Medical Corps for nonmedical personnel, and officers in these units did not enjoy the prestige of physicians. Psychologists often had to depend on the good will of the camp surgeon if their program was to achieve success.

Meanwhile regular military officers had many doubts about the psychological testing program. The army launched three investigations of it, which produced a number of criticisms and demonstrated that testing was poorly understood within the military. Many camp commanders, for example, did not differentiate between psychiatric and psychological examinations. Even though the investigations showed that psychologists were performing useful work, the General Staff in May 1918 was sufficiently distrustful of the program to refuse Yerkes's request for fifty-two more commissioned officers. Only in August, when the chief of staff issued a general order under which the program's psychologists could operate, did Yerkes point to "numerous indications that the tide has turned and that military opinion is rapidly becoming favorable to various lines of psychological work."[14]

Despite the difficulties, the army's intelligence testing program was the most massive effort of its kind ever undertaken. It examined over 1,725,000 men. The scores revealed 7,800 unfit for service and another 20,000 probably suited only for limited use. In addition personnel officers assigned recruits to various units partly on the basis of test results. The program employed some 100 officers (all of whom had been psychologists in civilian life) and 250 enlisted men (most of whom had been graduate students—in either psychology or education). The psychologists working for Yerkes showed that they could productively examine normal adults in large groups. The potential use of intelligence testing in peacetime thus grew immensely.

Yet many psychologists shared Yerkes's disappointment with the program. Military officials had never really accepted the work, and they terminated it only two months after the war ended.[15] Some psychologists chafed under the control of physicians and wondered why they had been assigned to the Medical Corps in the first place. Bitterness lingered for years in some men who had enlisted with the promise of a commission that Yerkes had subsequently been unable to procure. At the end of the war the army did pass along its thanks to Yerkes; but it awarded the Distinguished Service Medal to Scott. As they drifted back to civilian life, most psychologists agreed that intelligence testing was an aspect not of medicine but of personnel work. That they properly belonged in the Adjutant General's Office was a lesson they were not to forget.

The period immediately after the war brought important changes to applied psychology. Practitioners pushed the APA into taking action that might help them in their struggles against incompetents and charlatans. Clinical psychology expanded its horizons; industrial psychology won new popularity; and psychological testing became a source of public controversy.

During the war the distinction between experimental and applied psychology had become more obscure as many psychologists left their academic laboratories to work on military problems. Several hundred eventually participated in the war effort, either in uniform or as civilian consultants. But almost all of them continued to think of themselves as researchers, and they were reluctant to see the APA, originally dedicated to the advancement of science, become involved in professional issues. Cognizant of this opinion, some practitioners decided that their interests would best be served by a new national organization to supplement the APA. In 1917 the association faced the first threat to its supremacy since Titchener's abortive challenge thirteen years before.

At the APA's annual meeting in December 1917, seven of its members tentatively organized the American Association of Clinical Psychologists. Others who had been invited (Yerkes, for example) did not attend this first meeting for fear they would be considered schismatics. Forty-eight psychologists were elected charter members, all but two of whom later agreed to join. Dedication to the APA became apparent, however, at an unscheduled special session called to discuss the new organization. In a crowded and animated meeting most speakers opposed the formation of any group that might threaten the APA. The founders of the new association decided to put off formal organization for a year, but again in 1918 they found too much opposition to proceed.

In 1919 the rebellion ended. The APA set up a committee to consider certifying some APA members as "consulting psychologists." More important, it agreed to the establishment of a special clinical section to handle professional issues. Satisfied by these concessions, members of the American Association of Clinical Psychologists decided to dissolve their organization while it was still in its nebulous state and to reconstitute it as the APA's Clinical Section. The new group assigned itself three goals: promoting better working relationships within clinical psychology and with allied fields, developing professional standards for practitioners, and encouraging research and publication on topics in clinical psychology.

Thus, with great caution and reluctance the APA involved itself in professional issues. It remained to be seen what sort of certification program would emerge, or whether the Clinical Section could achieve its aims within an organization primarily interested in scientific problems. The association had made no concession to practitioners in its membership standards; on the contrary, in 1921 published research became an admission requirement for the first time. But the importance of applied psychology had been acknowledged; the walls of scholarly exclusiveness were soon to begin crumbling as well.

In addition to winning a partial victory within the APA, applied psychologists also saw new areas of practice open during the period immediately following the war. Clinical psychologists worked in army rehabilitation hospitals, where they found themselves in situations unlike any they had previously known. Their use there had begun during the war when Yerkes promoted it as an alternative form of service in case the testing program fell through. After the armistice about half of the men in Yerkes's program completed their enlistments working in rehabilitation. They treated each patient individually—interviewing, giving trade and intelligence tests, helping with learning problems of the handicapped, and trying to raise morale. Operating in all forty-three army hospitals, the program marked the most extensive use of the clinical method with adults that psychologists had yet undertaken.

Industrial psychologists came out of the war with increased prestige in the business community. At a time when many of the firms had not yet established personnel departments, Scott and coworkers clearly demonstrated the effectiveness of a centralized system to place employees. Vocational testing burgeoned after the war, becoming more of a fad than an applied science. By 1920 hundreds of companies had bought prefabricated tests and were using them with little care or understanding. In contrast, only about thirty firms carried on the kind of meticulous research required for a valid and reliable testing program. An increasing number of psychologists were employed as part-time advisors to businesses. An early but abortive attempt to organize these psychologists came in the formation of the Economic Psychology Association. Several prominent psychologists joined, but they soon developed doubts about the founder, who had little if any formal psychological training.[16] A more reputable organization was founded by Scott himself. In 1919 he established the Scott Company. Staffed by former members of the Committee on Classification of Personnel, it was America's first successful psychological consulting firm. In the next few years it did a brisk and lucrative business.

As was the case before the war, intelligence testing became laden with great social significance. Of all the psychologists' activities it was the one that most sharply struck public consciousness. Results from the army's testing program had been tabulated by race; when they were released they seemed to show the intellectual superiority of Nordics over eastern and southern Europeans. The average immigrant from England had a mental age of 14.87; from Holland, 14.32; and from Germany, 13.88. In contrast, the average Russian scored 11.34; the Italian, 11.01; and the Pole, 10.74. Under Goddard's classification the people in the latter group were morons. Those who led the effort to restrict immigration—and they were soon to be successful—eagerly publicized these figures as proof that American stock needed protection. Some psychologists agreed, but many others concluded that their work was being misinterpreted and that they themselves needed to rethink their ideas about intelligence and feeblemindedness.

Applied psychologists came a long way in the quarter-century after Witmer founded his clinic. Clinical psychology spread geographically; it branched out from learning difficulties to personality problems; and it began to treat adults as well as children. More and more, clinical psychologists found themselves in competition with psychiatrists, poorly trained testers, and complete charlatans. Meanwhile industrial psychologists expanded from early work in advertising to the more fruitful fields of personnel management and vocational testing. In only a few years they had gained the support and confidence of many businessmen; as they entered the twenties their problem was to fulfill what might prove to be unrealistically high expectations. Intelligence testers also made spectacular advances. Beginning with a few feeble-minded and delinquent children, they quickly came to the point of examining a large part of the army. Conceptual difficulties, however, obscured the value of their work, and controversy marked their progress.

If applied psychology was becoming established as a technical field, it remained in its childhood as a profession. The overwhelming proportion of its practitioners were academicians first and foremost. The army introduced many psychologists to the potential applications of their discipline, but most of them took these newly found interests back to the campus with them. The APA continued as a scholarly organization. The formation of the Clinical Section, however, portended a future in which applied psychologists would turn more toward professional issues.

Applied psychology spread in too many directions to permit its growth to be attributed to a single cause. Its rise was intimately connected to several of those social changes that Federick Jackson Turner had seen as characteristic of America after 1890. Turner called attention to the development of great cities. Applied psychology was primarily an urban phenomenon. Most of the practitioners lived in cities, and the problems they addressed—delinquency, unassimilated immigrants, nonconforming schoolchildren—were largely urban problems. Turner saw the formation of large industrial empires. With them came vast new management problems and a growing preoccupation with efficiency. Applied psychologists, with their widening variety of psychological tests, provided a timely management tool that attracted interest among the leaders of some of America's largest corporations. Turner also noted the growth of the federal government, a phenomenon that culminated in unprecedented centralized controls during the First World War. One example of the new government power, the military's decision to measure the psyches of its recruits, gave applied psychology a potent impetus that it could have received in no other way.

Finally Turner mentioned the disappearance of "the old pioneer individualism" and the rise of "the forces of social combination." It became increasingly important for Americans to subordinate personal goals to the needs of larger organizations. People had to be made to "fit in" without experiencing a demoralizing loss of free will. Applied psychologists seized upon this imperative of modern society. Especially in the decades after World War 1, they were to make help in personal adjustment their primary contribution to American society.

2

ADJUSTMENT
Science, Service, and Ideal

"A man's whole life consists in a process of adjustment to his environment. . . ."[1] A. T. Poffenberger made this observation in his book *Applied Psychology* (1927), and by the mid-twenties few American psychologists would have disagreed with him. Much of academic psychology involved studying the adjustment of man and other animals. The theoretical orientation of psychologists might differ, but this fundamental topic of concern remained the same.

Psychologists interested in the practical application of their discipline viewed adjustment as more than a topic of scholarly inquiry. They knew that if they were to achieve professional status they needed to claim successfully that they provided an important service to a large segment of the public. Without a wide field of application psychology might be recognized as a science but never as a profession. Broadly speaking, adjustment was the service the applied psychologists offered the public.

Having defined their service, applied psychologists needed to go two steps further to win public support. First, they had to stake a claim to exclusive competence. If psychiatrists, graphologists, or astrologers could do as well fitting people into their environment, then the training and

---

In sampling the writing of applied psychologists this chapter relies on books published between 1925 and 1938 which were not aimed at other psychologists. Textbooks in applied psychology and guides for behavior came under scrutiny, but monographs did not. For the purposes of this chapter an applied psychologist is a psychologist who identified himself with applied work to the extent that he joined the American Association for Applied Psychology and thus had his name listed in its *Directory of Applied Psychologists.* The chapter does not attempt to analyze the results of psychological research, even though such findings may give some indication of the psychologists' hopes and values. Their racist views, for example, are ignored on this basis.

techniques of applied psychology would possess no special merit. The applied psychologists had to explain why the public should turn to them rather than their competitors. Second, they needed to show that their service had widespread application. If only a few people could benefit from adjustment, then driving their rivals from the field would not guarantee applied psychologists a prosperous future. Applied psychology required a large base of support if it was to take its place with the established professions.

After the postwar enthusiasm for psychology died down, applied psychologists began to make a calm, rational appeal to the public. From the mid-twenties to the beginning of World War 2, applied psychologists made a coherent case for their competence and their usefulness to a variety of audiences. Parents, educators, businessmen, and college students all heard about the virtues of applied psychology. And beyond the logical argument—written between the lines of textbooks and popular manuals— was a vision of a better America, a well-adjusted society in which social utility merged with personal fulfillment to provide a satisfying life for all.

Applied psychologists staked their claim to exclusive competence on an identification with science. They tried to link their beliefs and activities with those of scientists, whose knowledge, fitness, and proficiency were beyond question. The period between the wars marked a golden age of the scientific world-view. Nature appeared to hold few mysteries beyond human understanding, and man himself became a new frontier for scientific investigation. Applied psychologists seldom felt compelled to justify the application of science to human problems. They never bothered to attack religion, for example, nor did they see themselves in competition with priests and ministers. Presumably people who sought aid and solace from the church could be ignored as a dwindling minority that was out of touch with the realities of modern life.

Applied psychologists did, however, object to practitioners who passed themselves off as scientists without displaying the trappings of science. Contrasting themselves to this source of competition, applied psychologists proudly cited their own use of the scientific method, laboratory experimentation, and statistical techniques. They attacked phrenologists, character analysts, and other purported "psychologists" who had no training in academic psychology and whose invalid techniques produced untrustworthy results. Sometimes applied psychologists devoted whole chapters of their books to distinguishing themselves from those they considered charlatans. They knew that their field would not gain popular acceptance as an applied science until the public ceased associating it with various forms of pseudoscience.

Unfortunately, the accomplishments of applied psychologists still fell short of their aspirations. They realized, for example, that a psychologist who was using an unreliable or invalid test was little more help to a school or business than a graphologist or some other pseudoscientist. Consequently applied psychologists displayed a becoming modesty when comparing their field to the established sciences. Psychology still had far to go, they explained, because it was the newest science. They remained optimistic, for they believed that psychology, moving with the tides of industrialization and expanding technology, like other applied sciences was making slow but irresistible advances throughout the world.

Applied psychologists believed that their discipline, like the physical sciences, had a responsibility not merely to describe and understand phenomena but to predict and control them as well. They thought that the major part of their duty as applied scientists involved placing techniques for the control of human behavior at the disposal of their clients and employers. Occasionally they had some qualms about the purposes to which their work might be put, and they realized that psychology could not appear as value-free as physics or chemistry. Still, applied psychologists remained loyal to their conception of natural science. They believed that ultimately the control of their fellow men would prove beneficial, for, as one textbook brightly exclaimed, "Everyone wants to know how to control other people."[2]

For the most part, applied psychologists were so certain of the beneficence of their work that they cheerfully volunteered to labor for anyone who was willing to pay their salaries and recognize their importance. The only time they cloaked themselves in scientific disinterest came when they explained their role in advertising. Applied psychologists believed that advertisements usually were useful and honest. They were well aware of exceptions, however, and they wanted to disclaim responsibility if their discoveries became the basis for deceptive advertising. "It is not within the province of the scientist to evaluate the effect of his investigations upon society," declared H. E. Burtt in *The Psychology of Advertising*. "Applied science, strictly speaking, is concerned with means rather than ends." But Burtt also suggested that as an individual, if not as a scientist, the psychologist ought to care about how his employers used his findings.[3] The raising of this endlessly difficult problem offered only a brief hint that applied psychologists felt some uneasiness in the role of the scientist.

American psychology arose from a fundamentally Darwinian base, and when applied psychologists talked about scientific theory they primarily meant evolutionary biology. One notion taken from Darwin stressed the variation of individuals within any population, animal or human. Applied psychologists believed that mental characteristics varied among humans just as physiological characteristics did. Psychological testing, in fact, was based on just this premise. Applied psychologists followed Darwin further by arguing that each individual acted so as to adapt himself to his surroundings. "One of the most basic generalizations of the biological sciences," observed Lawrence Shaffer in *The Psychology of Adjustment*, "is that all living organisms tend to vary their activities in response to changed conditions in their environment."[4]

In the twenties and thirties most educated Americans could easily accept this version of Darwinism. But there were some hidden premises to the argument. Early functionalist psychologists had contended that, like other organs, the mind had an adaptive purpose. Studying psychology meant studying individual adaptation, that is, trying to discover how the mind helped the human organism adjust to its environment. The emphasis on adjustment persisted even after many psychologists lost interest in the "mind" as something different from behavior. By the mid-twenties explicit functionalism had almost completely disappeared from the discussions presented by applied psychologists. Its ghost remained, however.

Applied psychologists took the notions of variation and adaptation from Darwinism, but they balked at the idea of the survival of the fittest. Applied psychologists were not Social Darwinists in the mold of William Graham Sumner, and they did not intend to spread the pessimistic doctrine that a certain proportion of humanity was destined to be mere wastage. At the turn of the century, when applied psychology was just beginning, many students of society had challenged the inhumane features of Social Darwinism. For example, John Dewey, one of the founders of functionalism, strongly believed that man need not be at the mercy of his environment but could change it to suit his purposes. Perhaps the sociologist Lester Ward came closest to the position later held by applied psychologists. Ward contended that in ongoing societies individual adjustment tended to preserve the social order. There was no reason to worry about sloughing off the unfit, because a method always existed to harmonize individual desires and social needs. Adjustment thus became a highly optimistic feature of the applied psychologists' version of Darwinism.

The identification of applied psychology with science included little discussion of philosophical or theoretical questions. Applied psychologists, for example, never defined psychology's special realm of inquiry. It was variously seen as behavior, habits, motives, feelings, or some combination of these. Most academic psychologists desired to come to some consensus on this issue, and they usually wrote from a clear theoretical viewpoint. The applied psychologists, on the other hand, while aware of theoretical questions, preferred to avoid them. Sometimes they presented various viewpoints; sometimes they denied the importance of a theoretical framework, arguing that their task was merely to achieve some practical result; sometimes they ignored such questions altogether. Applied psychologists believed that they could successfully claim to be scientists without first explaining the fundamental nature of their science. In a sense, they were forced into this pragmatic position, for they could not explain what they did not know.

Having founded their claim to exclusive competence on an identification with science, applied psychologists still needed to show that their basic service—aid in human adjustment—would draw a large clientele. The potential was surely vast, for psychologists believed that every person was continually adjusting himself to the environment. Because adjustment was a fundamental life process, however, it had been going on long before psychology came on the scene. In contending that people now needed help in adjustment, applied psychologists based their argument on the assumption that the environment was becoming so complex that the simple mechanisms and patterns of adjustment that people had used in the past no longer could prove effective. When they surveyed the American scene, applied psychologists pointed out the many pockets of maladjustment that required their services.

Applied psychologists hoped that adjustment, like charity, would begin at home. They believed that adult habits and behavior patterns were developed in early childhood. Parents thus had the primary responsibility for helping their children become competent and humane adults. Unfortunately, the family was failing to keep up with rapid and profound social changes because the values of the parents no longer formed an effective basis for the adjustments of their children. Americans, observed Lawrence Averill in *The Hygiene of Instruction* (1928), were living in "an age of extraordinary family and social unrest wherein the old restraints and safeguards of the home are proving wholly inadequate to orient boys and girls rationally and harmoniously to life and its unusual demands...."[5]

Parents needed help in producing well-adjusted children. Applied psychologists thought that they could be of service by familiarizing parents with the principles of child development and encouraging them to adopt a more objective attitude toward their children. Along this line two psychologists from the University of Minnesota published an "up-to-date, scientific, and useful" baby book, *Your Child, Year by Year*. The authors not only provided space for the child's height, weight, photographs, and so on, but they also included tests that measured muscular coordination, language proficiency, and intellectual capacity. They promised that such a record, continued until age sixteen, would be "important both from the scientific viewpoint and from the practical viewpoint of modifying and directing conduct."[6] Because they had no sure method to reach the majority of American parents, applied psychologists believed that they could have greater influence in the school than in the home. Here, by convincing only a small group of educational administrators, they might affect the adjustment patterns of a large number of children. In the classroom teachers had the opportunity to develop in their students the sort of mind that could produce an integrated personality by adjusting to changes in the environment. Not enough administrators and teachers, however, understood their responsibility for promoting the individual adjustment of each student. They failed to realize that their prime duty was to create a classroom environment that produced appropriate adjustments.

Applied psychologists thought that too many schools were still being operated under the notion that their main job was imparting knowledge. The schools failed to teach their students how to think creatively and constructively in new situations; they did not consider the differing needs and abilities of their students; and they placed undue emphasis on academic achievement. Pupils did not become well adjusted to school, and more important, they did not learn how to adjust to life. Applied psychologists, especially those interested in school problems, joined the movement for progressive education. They envisioned a major role for themselves in the transformation of the school.

A person formed his adjustment patterns at home and in the school, but it was at work that he finally put them to the test. Applied psychologists believed that someone's job—his adaptation to the occupational world—constituted the most important adjustment that he would ever try to make. Success on the job led not only to material rewards but to social esteem and personal satisfaction. It followed that someone poorly adjusted to his job had difficulty enjoying the rest of his activities. As the authors of *Psychology in Everyday Living* explained, "Happiness and effectiveness in nearly every other life function are dependent upon satisfactory occupational adjustment."[7] Here lay another vast field for the applied psychologists.

Finding the right job assumed enormous significance. "Choosing a vocation," declared Richard Wellington Husband of the University of Wisconsin, "is without doubt the most important decision a person ever makes during the course of his life."[8] Such a decision demanded the most careful and objective self-analysis, one that produced information on aptitudes, abilities, interests, and intelligence. Few people could gather all the necessary data on their own, but they risked disaster if they took a job without first knowing how successfully they would fit in. The applied psychologists, armed with a great variety of tests, were ready to solve this dilemma. They could furnish to an individual the personal data he needed in order to facilitate his advantageous adjustment in the most important aspect of his life—his work.

Applied psychologists had a fairly clear idea of the kind of jobholder that their services would produce. To begin with, the well-adjusted worker had genuine enthusiasm for his job. He became deeply involved in it, put in long hours, and believed that the work made him a better person. "Other things being halfway equal," declared Lawrence Averill in *The Hygiene of Instruction,* "the hard-working man is mentally sound and well-adjusted, while the lazy and idle man is equally unsound and ill-adjusted."[9] All jobs could become interesting and enjoyable, and the well-adjusted worker found challenges in them that his discontented colleagues ignored. He discovered opportunities in seemingly menial tasks. The well-adjusted typist, to quote the author of *Finding Yourself in Your Work,* "learned to grow through the typing situation."[10] Applied psychologists expected that successful occupational adjustment would result in an intense, almost fervid, commitment to the job.

Although applied psychologists concentrated their attention on the individual worker, they were clearly offering a service to industrial managers as well. Few things could be better for business than a work force of well-adjusted employees. Because adjustment and diligence were reciprocal characteristics, applied psychologists found a fundamental compatibility between happiness and productivity. "The industrial psychologist," explained Morris S. Viteles of the University of Pennsylvania, "is primarily concerned with the individual at work in the belief that, in the final analysis, the maximum efficiency of that individual in the industrial situation can only be achieved by insuring his most satisfactory adjustment in that situation."[11] This was a strong selling point with the businessman, who might fear that promoting adjustment would necessarily raise costs; applied psychologists assured him that, on the contrary, a well-adjusted work force would increase his profits.

While sympathizing with the worker, the applied psychologists seldom tried to put their talents at the disposal of labor unions. They never explained how psychology could be applied to produce successful strikes, organizational drives, or collective bargaining. Nevertheless, applied psychologists considered labor unions an understandable response by workers to their problems. As long as management refused to promote the adjustment of its employees, it must face the annoyance of unions. Only when it adopted a more humane notion of work could it expect to bring labor organizations under its control. For their part union leaders expressed little demand for the services of applied psychologists. Stressing higher wages, shorter hours, and similar issues, unions failed to understand that the true cause of worker discontent was occupational maladjustment. Nor did applied psychologists see potential allies among the laborers themselves. Because of the educational, intellectual, and esthetic inferiority of the average industrial worker, he comprehended the psychological causes of his unhappiness even less thoroughly than misguided union organizers or myopic businessmen.

Applied psychologists also offered services to adults whose maladjustments were not entirely occupational. The whole purpose of clinical psychology was to realign adjustment mechanisms to allow an individual to fit in better to his environment. People with less serious problems could help themselves. In *Vocational Self Guidance*, for instance, Douglas Fryer wrote a chapter telling his readers that they still had an opportunity for "choosing a personality."[12] As people got older, conceded Sadie Myers Shellow in *How to Develop Your Personality*, they found it took greater effort to "correct undesirable personality traits." But with self-analysis and the application of psychological principles, they would find it "a painless and indeed a pleasant task."[13] The applied psychologist held out hope to the unhappy and dissatisfied: they could have a new life if they came to understand their unsuccessful adjustment mechanisms and genuinely wanted to change them.

Applied psychologists envisioned a vast clientele for their services. Aiming their appeal at both managers and individuals, they believed they could be of help to literally everyone in the country. Nevertheless, they limited their services somewhat by concentrating, perhaps unintentionally, on the white urban male. Members of minority groups received no advice on how to adjust to prejudice and discrimination, although those who were trying to assimilate into a larger society might have discovered some useful tips. Working women got little attention, probably for the reason that they appeared destined for motherhood and consequently were unable to make the intense commitment to their jobs that characterized well-adjusted male workers. Housewives were ignored altogether, and because applied psychology aimed to adjust people to an industrialized, bureaucratic, and essentially urban environment, farmers and others who lived in rural settings also received no special notice. Even with these limitations, however, applied psychologists made the sort of broad claims for their services that were prerequisites to professional status.

Applied psychologists based their claim to professional status on the dispassionate performance of a scientifically based social service. Beneath the rationality and altruism, however, lay a stratum of hopes, biases, and opinions that did not logically follow from scientific premises. Although these ideas took no coherent form and received no systematic presentation, they were still there, only partly hidden between the lines of textbooks and popular manuals. Like the already recognized professions, applied psychology had something that could pass for its own unique ideology. Applied psychologists held beliefs about economics, politics, and a better social order that separated them from other groups claiming to perform psychological services.

The key to their economic thought was a denial that either capitalism or industrialism necessarily estranged men from their labor. "Work," declared Morris S. Viteles, "is not a commodity—a mere inanimate element in the process of manufacture." On the contrary, it was "inseparable from the personality of the worker."[14] The growth of blue collar and other tedious jobs had indeed diminished opportunities for self-expression, but the effects of this loss could be offset by actions of business management: placing people in the most suitable jobs, responding to their needs, and generally making their work as pleasant as possible. Too often, however, management shortsightedly pursued profits and disregarded the welfare of its workers. "This heartlessness, this impersonality, of industry," predicted Percival M. Symonds of Teachers College at Columbia University, "will some day be looked upon as a great social crime."[15]

Applied psychologists cared less about the nature of the economic system than about the adjustment of the workers. They believed that capitalism could be reformed by changing the attitudes of business management. They launched no attack on the idea of private property, nor did they question the distinction between employer and employee. The depression of the 1930s, however, shook some of the applied psychologists' faith in the American economic system. Unemployment and poverty gave the workers a legitimate grievance, and business management had to act to win back their allegiance. Otherwise, applied psychologists were ready to see major structural changes in the economy. "The nature of the economic system," warned Harry Walker Hepner in *Human Relations in Changing Industry*, "is less important than the extent to which the system gives the worker opportunity for a sense of worthful participation."[16]

Applied psychologists had even more serious doubts about the American political system. Although they never said so explicitly, they saw contradictions between democracy and psychology. Psychological tests demonstrated profound differences among individuals which called into question the egalitarian premise of the governmental system. Some people possessed the aptitude and intelligence for leadership, while others did not even meet the standards of an informed voter. All people were not created equal, and it was unscientific to pretend they were. Moreover, applied psychologists had little respect for the judgment of the common man. Many people led disorganized lives; they lacked foresight and allowed mere luck to rule their existences. Individuals acted too often on emotion, and in a group they became illogical and impetuous. Meanwhile perhaps half of America's workers, having chosen their jobs unscientifically, were now pitifully unable to cope with their lives. Applied psychologists doubted whether a nation full of maladjusted individuals could elect those best suited for leadership.

Nevertheless, applied psychologists discounted the communist and fascist alternatives to liberal democracy. Left-wingers posed the more serious domestic challenge, so they received particular scorn. "Many a communist," explained Harry Walker Hepner of Syracuse University, "merely projects his own difficulties against the symbolized authority of the established government or business system." Radicals, he believed, were "slightly sick people who should be treated scientifically rather than feared." They could be cured if their real problems were exposed. The average communist "should be invited to visit a counselor in order that he may be shown how to make adjustments in the form of balanced, intelligent attempts to improve his own life before he undertakes to improve the government of peoples."[17] Advocating left-wing political beliefs thus resembled throwing temper tantrums or biting fingernails: all signaled poor adjustment.

Implicit in this criticism was a tendency not to take any ideas at face value. Applied psychologists had no interest, for example, in whether the radical view of American society was accurate. They believed the important question was whether such ideas produced maladjustive behavior. Radicalism showed only that some people were having adjustment problems. On the other hand, conservatism could stake no claim to immutable truth either. Such ideas might fit best into the American environment, but they could prove maladjustive elsewhere. Applied psychologists thus established adjustment as the standard by which political and economic ideas were to be judged.

Applied psychologists evaluated individuals by a similar criterion, and they thought they found some common characteristics in well-adjusted people. Such persons were independent, self-reliant, and optimistic; they felt confident about the present social order and expected things to improve in the future. They planned ahead and scorned merely living for the moment. They knew that nothing came easily and accepted the idea that life was a struggle. They acted cooperatively and sympathetically with their friends and acquaintances. They behaved thoughtfully and judiciously; they might be enthusiastic but were never overly emotional. Some might question whether such paragons of Victorian morality would actually fit so comfortably into an American society that was supplementing the Protestant work ethic with values arising from leisure and consumption. In listing the concomitants of adjustment, applied psychologists seemed to be describing the kind of people they liked and admired rather than making scientific generalizations.

Adjustment also led applied psychologists to their dream of a better world. Perhaps every true profession has such a dream, in which it imagines what would happen if it could perfect its skills and expand its services. Doctors might foresee a time when disease had completely disappeared; lawyers might envision a society in which liberty and justice were available to all; engineers might imagine a world where all resources were put to their most efficient use. At any rate, for applied psychologists a better America meant a well-adjusted society. What they dimly foresaw was a sophisticated meritocracy in which the most apt leaders would implement policies that maximized the adjustment of each citizen.

Applied psychologists wanted every American to have his own niche in society, one that he found important and satisfying. But they believed that before social institutions could provide a special place for each individual, they needed far more complete information about him than they now had. When collected, these data would be used by schools, businesses, and government to situate everyone properly. Equity rather than equality of opportunity would rule; each individual would progress as far as his capacities allowed. Floyd L. Ruch of the University of Southern California found a motto for the ideal state in a Biblical parable about the Last Judgment: "To him that hath shall be given."[18] Meanwhile multiple standards of success would be developed so that those people without the aptitude and intelligence to lead would still feel a sense of accomplishment. The kind of elitism favored by applied psychologists would produce no resentment. Of course, it would not allow much privacy either, for everyone's attitudes and behavior would need to be closely monitored.

In exchange for the loss of privacy, applied psychologists promised what utopian thinkers had long sought—the disappearance of individual and group conflict. A person who learned to respond effectively to every change in his environment and operated in settings that maximized his sense of satisfaction would experience a lasting feeling of inner peace. Applied psychologists insisted that hostile emotions and behavior were not directly produced by the environment but grew from within the individual as a result of faulty patterns of adjustment. It followed, to quote the author of *Personality Maladjustments and Mental Hygiene,* that "were the earth peopled with more harmonious and better integrated personalities, there would be less political and social conflict. . . ."[19] Groups would not contend with one another, because they possessed no needs and desires distinct from those of their members. Well-adjusted people meant the end of group conflict.

The applied psychologists never explained how the well-adjusted society would come into being, however. They faced something of a dilemma, for although they took little interest in the process of social change, they nevertheless criticized institutions for pursuing improper goals. Schools were imparting knowledge and businesses were increasing productivity when they should have been trying primarily to assure the maximum adjustment of each student and worker. Applied psychologists knew that institutions needed changing, but they also believed that anyone who acted to change them must be maladjusted. Since plans for change arose from poor adjustment, they could not be taken seriously. Instead, the discontented required counseling to determine the psychological roots of their dissatisfaction. Applied psychologists wanted changes, but they did not trust the maladjusted to implement them. The road to a better world seemed to have no starting point.

Only one group had sufficient knowledge and disinterest to promote institutional change—the applied psychologists themselves. Acting as something of an evolutionary cadre, they would work within institutions to convert administrators to the virtues of adjustment. Since the imperatives of modern society seemed to be acting in their behalf, applied psychologists felt assured of their ultimate success. Under their tutelage the well-adjusted society would emerge gradually but irresistibly. Meanwhile everyone else could concentrate on his own personal adjustment problems and leave social change to the psychological experts. Implicitly at least, applied psychologists asked the public to have confidence not merely in their knowledge and skills but in their ability to construct a better world as well.

Essentially applied psychologists believed that if everyone were well adjusted, social problems would disappear because no one would be left to perceive them. If the United States had been a well-adjusted society in 1937, for example, President Roosevelt never would have sought aid for the millions of Americans who were ill housed, ill clad, and ill nourished: neither he nor they would have had any concern about their condition. In reality, however, people did care about their social environment. Americans remained poorly adjusted, and the applied psychologist had little power to alter this fact on his own. He had to work for employers whose hearts might not be stirred by his vision of a better world and whose hopes for mankind might be less altruistic than his own. Adjustment, designed to find a place for everyone, could easily become a justification for keeping everyone in his place. Applied psychologists occasionally saw people playing an active role in adjustment, but for the most part they wrote as if the environment were fixed and beyond the control of the individual. In this sense adjustment and its ramifications provided a conservative response to rapid changes in American society.

3

THE PERILS OF POPULARITY

The United States, observed humorist Stephen Leacock in 1924, was suffering from an "outbreak of psychology." "In earlier days," he explained, "this science was kept strictly confined to the colleges" where "it had no particular connection with anything at all, and did no visible harm to those who studied it." But all that changed when new research showed that psychology could be used "for almost everything in life." "There is now," Leacock continued, "not only psychology in the academic or college sense, but also a Psychology of Business, a Psychology of Education, a Psychology of Salesmanship, a Psychology of Religion, a Psychology of Boxing, a Psychology of Investment, and a Psychology of Playing the Banjo." People called on the services of a psychologist as naturally as those of a plumber. "In all our great cities there are already, or soon will be, signs that read 'Psychologist—Open Day and Night.'"[1]

Historian William E. Leuchtenburg agrees. In the years after World War 1, he writes, "psychology became a national mania."[2] Consciousness, rationality, will, and the other characteristics of the mind that had underpinned much of psychology and most of common sense before the war fell into disrepute. Many Americans became disillusioned with the outcome of the war. The slaughter, the political upheavals, and the final settlement appeared far removed from the well-conceived plans of either soldiers or statesmen. It seemed that new ideas about motivation and behavior were in order. Meanwhile psychologists had been developing theories that fit in nicely with the postwar temper. Both psychoanalysis and behaviorism derogated consciousness and its concomitants. The former denied their importance; the latter, their existence.

Sigmund Freud had come to the United States in 1909, and the visit had sparked interest in psychoanalytic psychology. Even before the war his theories, although imperfectly understood and often taken out of context, had won adherents among some psychiatrists, psychologists, and intellectuals. It was in the twenties, however, that the flood of Freudianism burst upon American society. Millions of people began sprinkling their conversations with "repression," "libido," "Oedipus complex," and the other exciting terms of the psychoanalytic lexicon. Because of his emphasis on sex Freud was seen as placing a scientific imprimatur on the destruction of Victorian morality. Although relatively few people had either the money or the opportunity to undergo psychoanalytic treatment, anyone could buy one of the outpouring of new books of Freudianism. Even Sears, Roebuck began retailing Freud; its catalog offered customers *Ten Thousand Dreams Interpreted* and *Sex Problems Solved.*

Freud's system enjoyed much less popularity among American psychologists than among the public at large. Psychologists were naturally distressed because many people who embraced Freud misunderstood him and saw in his attempts to be rational and scientific a license for the irrational and disorderly. But more than that, most American psychologists, raised in laboratories and committed to experimentation, found Freudianism out of temper with the kind of psychology they knew and believed in. Few if any American psychologists became psychoanalysts, although those applied psychologists who had the opportunity to treat patients did find some of Freud's ideas helpful. Psychoanalysis had greater influence on psychiatry; indeed, despite Freud's opposition, physicians were moving to make it their own exclusive realm.

Behaviorism, although wielding less influence on the public than psychoanalysis, was much more congenial to American psychology. If psychologists were not completely ready to abandon consciousness and encompass all human activity in the mechanisms of stimulus and response, they were at least impressed that behaviorism had a thoroughly experimental basis. Furthermore, its creator, John B. Watson, was a fellow countryman—in fact, a one-time president of the American Psychological Association and for many years a professor at Johns Hopkins. In the first edition of his book, *Psychology from the Standpoint of a Behaviorist,* published in 1913, Watson made an academic presentation of fairly restrained environmentalism. In 1920 he was forced to leave Johns Hopkins after an extramarital love affair with his research assistant erupted in a scandalous divorce. Deeply alienated from academe, Watson joined the J. Walter Thompson advertising agency in 1921, soon becoming a vice president.

After Watson's entrance into advertising his behaviorism became more

radical and more popular. He proclaimed the environment the only significant factor determining human behavior. Heredity and most instincts
joined consciousness in the psychological junkpile. Watson also delineated
more clearly the social implications of his system. He favored something
called "behavioristic freedom": the behaviorist, he explained, "would
like to develop his world of people from birth on, so that their speech
and their bodily behavior could equally well be exhibited freely every-
where without running afoul of group standards."[3] More and more Watson
forsook psychological research and scholarly journals; instead, he concentrated on propagating his simplified and optimistic doctrines in popular
magazines. His notions of child rearing, for example, not only inhabited
the pages of *Collier's* and *Cosmopolitan*, but they also formed the basis
of a top-selling government pamphlet, "Infant and Child Care."

To a large extent Freud and the later Watson remained outside the
mainstream of American psychology. The popularity of their doctrines
rubbed off on psychologists who were in no way responsible for them.
But the "national mania" for psychology had another root as well: intelligence testing. The testing program during World War 1 had given some
4 million men their first taste of psychology. After the war countless
thousands of job seekers found themselves faced with tests to determine
their probable proficiency. Testing, behaviorism, and psychoanalysis thus
brought to psychology a degree of public acceptance that it had never had
before and that in large measure it did not earn. The burgeoning popularity brought problems especially to applied psychologists.

Popularity in itself need not threaten a profession. For example,
when faced with an upsurge in public enthusiasm after World War 2,
psychologists were in a position to turn it to their own advantage. But
applied psychology was far from being a profession in 1920, and applied
psychologists found themselves trapped in a vicious circle of inadequacies
with no easy means to escape. The number of Americans who wanted
psychology to help them with one problem or another far exceeded
the number of psychologists who were prepared to do so. Frauds and
popularizers quickly filled the gap between demand and supply, and the
term "psychologist" came to mean anyone from a Binet tester to a mental
telepathist.

Moreover, when the fakers and the Sears, Roebuck manuals failed to
bring results, psychology received the blame. Donald G. Paterson lamented
from Minnesota that "in the quack-infested Northwest . . . the merits of
psychological research and application are imperiled by this wide spread
exploitation of pseudo-psychology."[4] Dorothy Yates of San Jose State
Teachers College wrote an entire book, *Psychological Racketeers*, in an

attempt to warn the public of frauds masquerading in the guise of psychologists. "There *is*," she assured her readers, "a body of sound information concerning mental life and human behavior, which is, in the true sense, a science." "And," she continued, "there *is* a genuine applied psychology."[5]

Although no means existed to ban popular psychology from the mails, end the numberless self-help courses, or silence the charlatans, applied psychologists could still hope one day to achieve a legal exclusivity of practice such as doctors enjoyed. If the state would distinguish between the applied psychologists and the frauds, the problem of legitimacy would be solved. Although the twenties witnessed some progress along this line, most psychologists considered it more practical to find a self-imposed method for signifying the real psychologists. A national certifying agency, if it had sufficient power and prestige, might be even more effective in assuring uniform high standards than forty-eight state legislatures. This was the approach that attracted applied psychologists after World War 1.

Before psychologists could begin certifying themselves, they needed to agree on the criteria they would use. This presented several related difficulties. There arose the question of how much training and experience a genuine psychologist needed to have. If, for example, a master's degree were set as the minimum standard, then many psychologists would be deprived of the additional status and prestige accruing to the doctorate. Moreover, psychologists would be permanently placed in an inferior position to psychiatrists and other physicians, all of whom had doctor's degrees. On the other hand, if the doctorate became the minimum qualification then hundreds of people who had been performing psychological work without such training must either lose their jobs or (far more likely) come to be called by some new title.

Even if psychologists did decide that a certifiable practitioner needed a doctorate—and that seemed to be the most prevalent opinion among those interested in certification during the twenties—there remained the question of what doctoral training ought to include. Psychology was a broad discipline, and students might concentrate on its philosophical, pedagogical, or physiological aspects. Clearly, the doctorate alone gave no indication of what its recipient knew, nor did it constitute a guarantee of competence. Furthermore, only a handful of graduate departments offered special programs in applied psychology, and they provided no uniformity of training. Finally, some psychologists suggested that desirable personality characteristics might be just as important for a practitioner as advanced degrees. No amount of technical knowledge, they argued, could make up for inability to develop rapport with clients.

If and when it arrived, certification must mean more than a guarantee of training and competence. It needed also to be a sign of continuing discretion and trustworthiness. Applied psychologists required a way to police themselves. They needed a code of ethics, a means of enforcing the code, and sure penalties for those who transgressed it. A charlatan offered misused clients no recourse against himself. A genuine psychologist, on the other hand, must be ready to jeopardize his entire career as a guarantee of his activities.

Before psychologists could solve any of their numerous problems of professionalization, they needed to form a national organization that was devoted to the practice of psychology. Only this kind of group could certify practitioners, coordinate campaigns for legislation, promote and standardize psychological training, and insure reliable practice. The organizational efforts of applied psychologists thus assumed much importance. The success of these efforts alone would not insure the growth of professional psychology—also required were useful technical skills and a large number of committed practitioners, for example—but failure to organize nationally would surely retard the development of the profession. In the twenties applied psychologists hoped to use the Clinical Section of the APA as the springboard for professional activity.

American psychiatrists, especially those working outside of mental institutions, formed one roadblock to these professional aspirations. Like psychologists, they faced many problems because of the expanding popularity of their field. They too needed to organize, develop standards of training, and combat the frauds and incompetents who were drawn to psychoanalysis. Psychiatrists favored only a subordinate role for applied psychologists in the treatment of mental disorders. In the previously uncharted territory of human maladjustment, psychiatrists attempted to stake out a wide area of exclusive competence. Conflict with applied psychologists became inevitable. After World War 1, then, the "national mania" for psychology promoted and intensified the struggle for "living space" between psychiatrists and psychologists. The applied psychologists thus were forced to use some of their meager resources in a struggle with this determined group of physicians.

Academic psychologists experienced few difficulties from the growing popularity of their discipline. They had entrenched themselves too well in their colleges and universities to be seriously threatened by the assault of frauds and popularizers. Scholarly credentials for psychologists followed the pattern established in other academic fields; additional certification was unnecessary. Because graduate programs in psychology were designed to produce academicians, no problem of standardized training arose. The professional questions that did bother academic psychologists—tenure, class load, or academic freedom, for example—related to their position as professors rather than as psychologists. These problems might be resolved through interdisciplinary groups such as the American Association of University Professors. Finally, academic psychologists already had in the APA a well-established national organization that served their scholarly interests. Applied psychologists were thus to find their academic colleagues uncertain allies in the struggle to attain professional status.

Growing popular interest in psychology coupled with a general rise in college admissions produced increased undergraduate and graduate enrollments during the twenties. Doctoral programs expanded, and the number of doctorates awarded in psychology rose sharply in the years after 1921. In 1930 twice as many Americans held Ph.D.s in psychology as had done so ten years before. The expansion of academic departments absorbed an overwhelming proportion of the new psychologists. For example, although the number of psychologists in the APA more than doubled between 1920 and 1930, the percentage without an academic affiliation increased only slightly. The job market for psychologists was thus closely tied to academic expansion. As long as the demand from colleges and universities remained strong, most new psychologists would obtain positions in higher education.

While applied psychology did not attract an increasing proportion of recent doctorates in the twenties, it did draw new psychologists in ever-expanding numbers. As the decade continued, women came to comprise a growing percentage of applied psychologists. Because of traditional prejudices against women in higher education, new academic positions for them did not keep pace with the number of doctorates they received. Many women psychologists found themselves in applied work because academic careers that were open to men remained closed to them.

A curious situation arose that did not augur well for the professionalization of applied psychology. Men comprised over two-thirds of all American psychologists in 1930, but they made up a distinct minority of applied psychologists. There did not exist in 1930 (nor does there exist today) a full-fledged profession that was composed mostly of women. Many factors go to explain this phenomenon, but one may well have been the reluctance of men to acknowledge that women could have professional status except in primarily male occupations. Even without consciously discriminating against them men may have categorized applied psychologists as subprofessionals like social workers and elementary school teachers simply because most practitioners were women. Convincing proof of this does not exist, but the suspicion remains that an influx of men into applied psychology would have enhanced the field's prospects for professional status.

In addition to the general problems that all applied psychologists faced in the period between World War 1 and the depression, each field of application—industrial, educational, and clinical—experienced the effects of expanding popularity in its own way. Taken together, separate events occurring in each branch form a picture of some progress and much frustration.

The success of the army's psychological testing program in World War 1 encouraged many American businessmen to believe that scientific methods could be applied to the problem of selecting workers with the highest potential. Psychologists were eager to help, and in the period following the war they developed a great number of selection tests. Some of these tests were based on careful research into specific problems, but many were produced hurriedly with small consideration of how they would be used. In addition, people with little psychological training were inventing tests and passing them off as scientific instruments. The unrealistically high expectations of businessmen soon combined with the general ineffectiveness of the tests to put an end to the testing boom. The early twenties saw businessmen abandon tests in droves; estimates of the defection rate ranged as high as 90 percent.

In 1925 Morris S. Viteles, then a consultant for the Philadelphia Yellow Cab and Rapid Transit Companies as well as an instructor at the University of Pennsylvania, told his colleagues that they must use a new approach if they were to win back their prestige among businessmen. Testing, he argued, was more complicated and more expensive than psychologists had claimed; it took more than a clerk in the employment department to administer a test successfully. Beyond test scores a business needed some knowledge of an individual's total personality to make a valid judgment about him. "In the cause of greater scientific accuracy in vocational selection in industry," Viteles stated, "the statistical point of view must be supplemented by a clinical point of view."[6]

While psychologists were having second thoughts about tests, they faced a serious challenge from a variety of pseudoscientists who also claimed to be able to provide benefits for businesses. One survey found a system called "character analysis" to be the most prevalent form of charlatanry. It was based on the notion that physical characteristics necessarily reflected personality qualities. Thus, the argument ran, because blonds were more aggressive than brunets, they made better salesmen. Many businessmen could not distinguish such nonsense from real psychology; when pseudoscientific methods failed, psychologists received the blame. Psychologists were not merely attacking straw men when they took up so much space in their popular works exposing and denouncing the frauds and fakers. The pseudoscientists had done much damage and posed a continuing threat.

One effective response to the charlatans came in the form of the Psychological Corporation, organized in 1921 by James McKeen Cattell. Its shareholders were all reputable psychologists who pledged to perform services for the corporation which would increase the value of the stocks. Psychology was offered for sale to any individual or group that had the money to pay for it. The most important clients were, of course, businesses. After a shaky start in the twenties the Psychological Corporation was to become well established; its annual gross receipts would climb beyond $1 million in the period after World War 2.

In addition to endowing industrial psychology with the aura of legitimate business, the Psychological Corporation acted as an agency of certification. Cattell explained in 1923 that only psychologists who met APA membership qualifications—a Ph.D., published research, and ongoing work in the field—could perform under the auspices of the corporation. The board of directors, who made up a veritable Who's Who of American psychology, added prestige to the organization. Moreover, the corporation had compiled "a black list of charlatans and ignoramuses, and a gray list of camp followers" who were deliberately excluded from its ranks. A client could be assured of psychological work of the highest quality. "The Corporation," Cattell explained, "guarantees the training and standards of those associated with it."[7]

Of the three fields of psychological application, industrial psychology remained closest to its academic roots. During the twenties only a handful of psychologists abandoned the campus for full-time work in industry. Industrial psychologists had no desire to change this situation, so part-time consulting—concentrating in the study of job requirements, vocational selection, and merchandising—became the usual vehicle for industrial psychology. Because of the reliance on academic credentials certification, such as that done by the Psychological Corporation, provided much less difficulty in industrial psychology than in other fields of application.

In the late twenties industrial psychologists faced an even greater threat than that posed by the competition of the charlatans or the ineffectiveness of their own techniques. A fundamental premise of industrial psychology, that productivity depended on how well a worker fit his job, came strongly into question as a result of research done at the Hawthorne Works of the Western Electric Company. Beginning innocuously in 1924 as a study of the effects of lighting on output, the research eventually pointed to the conclusion that the norms and values of workers' groups were what determined productivity. An individual's performance thus could not be predicted on the basis of test scores alone. Psychologists could not successfully challenge these findings, and in the thirties industrial sociology emerged to supplement industrial psychology.

In many respects events in educational psychology during the period after World War 1 paralleled those in the industrial field. The enthusiasm for testing among educators was even wider and deeper than among businessmen. The intelligence test, which had begun its career among mental defectives and then enjoyed a profitable enlistment in the army, came to its ultimate resting place, the classroom, in the postwar era. Group tests, inexpensively obtained and easily administered, tempted educators with the prospects of a more efficient school. Patterned after the Army Alpha, at least forty-two such tests were available by 1922. Intelligence testing had become more than applied psychology; it was now a big business as well. Estimates of the number of school children examined in 1920-21 ranged from a few hundred thousand to 2 million. The figures indicated two things. The numbers themselves showed that the schools were embarking on a testing program that rivaled the one the army had just completed, and the range of estimates demonstrated that neither psychologists nor educators were keeping a close watch on developments in the field of testing.

Intelligence testing also blossomed in college education. Administrators of elite private institutions, where the applicants outnumbered the available openings, began to use the tests to help them decide who ought to be admitted. In addition, examination scores provided a tool for educational guidance once a student had enrolled. Surveys in the early twenties revealed that about half of American colleges were utilizing the tests for some purpose; the proportion was higher among private institutions. Responding to this increased interest, the College Entrance Examination Board supplemented its achievement tests with the Scholastic Aptitude Test in 1926. Two years later the American Council on Education developed a test that found such ready acceptance as a device to measure college freshmen that in ten years the annual distribution came to exceed a quarter-million.

The accelerating popularity of intelligence testing did not indicate that psychologists had resolved the conceptual anomalies that the army program had uncovered. There remained the question of how much influence the environment had on test scores. Most psychologists still believed that I.Q. somehow indicated native intelligence, but by 1930 they had backed off a bit from their racist conclusions. Southern and eastern Europeans gained equality with Nordics; blacks, however, did not. Meanwhile some psychologists were beginning to express doubts about the unitary nature of intelligence, arguing that the Binet test and its successors measured only one aspect of mental capability. Psychologists never reached agreement on what (if anything) intelligence was and to what extent the I.Q. test measured it.[8]

Theoretical difficulties failed to stifle the enthusiasm for intelligence testing in the schools, however. There were several reasons why educators, unlike businessmen, never gave up on tests. To begin with, educational psychologists did not have to contend with the charlatan nor take responsibility for his failures. Virtually every teacher and school administrator had taken psychology courses and could distinguish genuine psychology from its fraudulent pretenders. The close alliance within academe between psychology and education meant that psychologists could usually count on the school, more than any other American institution, to provide a sympathetic hearing before an unskeptical audience. The problems with the concept of intelligence, moreover, seldom reached the public. Psychologists preferred to talk only to each other—or to say nothing at all.

Meanwhile the intelligence test offered educators something that would quicken the heartbeat of any administrator: a device to help in a more rational and efficient organization of the school. Unlike most tests in industry, intelligence tests had some predictive value—not because they measured intelligence but because they indicated scholastic potential. Of all human abilities psychologists had found it easiest to measure the ability to take tests. As schools consolidated in the twenties and thirties, the tendency to place students in classes according to ability grew. A survey in 1932 showed that 60 percent of schools with over five hundred pupils were using the intelligence test to group students. Test scores also provided an allegedly scientific, mathematical explanation for teachers' inability to educate certain children; those with low I.Q.s were not expected to learn much. "So far as the schools themselves are concerned," reported the *American School Board Journal* in 1931, "there is no serious question about the value of the intelligence quotient."[9]

Psychologists thus filled the demand for intelligence tests, but they did it at a high cost to professionalism. Tests were invented and distributed on the premise that almost anyone could administer them. The professional claim of exclusive technical competence became impossible to sustain in much of the use of psychology in the schools; egalitarianism prevailed. Meanwhile educational psychologists, secure in the higher circles of the academic world, did little to bridge the gap between themselves and the people in schools who gave individual tests, counseled students, set up testing programs, and performed other activities that might have been termed psychological. The 1930 APA *Year Book* revealed that psychological workers in schools were almost completely alienated from academic psychology. Of the many who were eligible to join the organization, only twenty-four psychologists employed by schools or school boards belonged to the APA.

One institution that linked organized academic psychology to the school was the "psycho-educational clinic." Its precedent lay in Lightner Witmer's facility at the University of Pennsylvania, which was founded in 1896 and was still going strong in the twenties. Usually affiliated with a university or school system, these clinics gave individual attention to the educational difficulties of specific students. They also became involved in conduct problems, pupil guidance, and cases of mental defect and abnormality. Their distinguishing feature was that, while psychiatrists, other physicians, social workers, and researchers might be on the staff, a psychologist always served as clinic director. This characteristic was to provide a continuing source of controversy with psychiatrists throughout the postwar era.

A survey in the early thirties found eighty-seven psycho-educational clinics operating in the United States. Those connected to colleges and universities were more numerous, smaller, and staffed by more Ph.D.s than those attached to schools. Psychologists in the latter group met high standards of training, however, with a large majority holding advanced degrees. Nonetheless, only seventeen school systems afforded their psychologists the facilities and thus the independence and prestige of a clinic. The distribution of psycho-educational clinics formed a very spotty picture. Some school systems—those in Chicago, Cleveland, and New York, for example—operated extremely active clinics that examined thousands of students annually, whereas others—those in St. Louis, San Francisco, or Milwaukee, for instance—had no clinic at all. So it was for universities, social agencies, prisons, and other institutions: for reasons that defy generalization, some sponsored clinics and some did not. Optimistic psychologists might find in this situation a great potential for expanded psychological demand.

Meanwhile the growth of clinical psychology outside educational institutions faced increasing opposition in the years after World War 1. In the clinical field psychologists encountered not only the amorphous threat of popularization but sometimes the organized resistance of another group of fledgling professionals—the psychiatrists. Clinical psychologists, declared J. E. Wallace Wallin, "were fighting for the recognition of certain basic professional ideals, particularly for professional status commensurate with their profession."[10] Confronted with the possibility of permanent subordination in an important and growing field, they—more than other applied psychologists—attempted to band together to secure opportunities for their advancement. The persistent conflict with psychiatrists did much to make clinical psychologists the advance guard in the professionalization of applied psychology. It is a position they have maintained for over fifty years.

The opposition of psychiatrists had grown quickly. In the early years of the century psychiatrists still spent most of their time in the treatment of mental patients confined to institutions. In 1908 a former inmate, Clifford W. Beers, published *The Mind That Found Itself.* A plea for the prevention of mental disease as well as for better care in asylums, the book launched the mental hygiene movement in the United States. A year later Beers founded the National Committee for Mental Hygiene to mobilize public support. While social thinkers, philanthropists, and some psychologists joined the movement, psychiatrists provided its guidance. The belief prevailed that the prevention and treatment of conduct disorders were medical problems and that only physicians should have responsibility for them.

In the years before American entry into the war, the National Committee promoted the establishment of psychopathic wards and outpatient clinics in hospitals. It also began a nationwide survey of mental health facilities. During World War 1 psychiatrists grew in stature. Their duty in eliminating the insane from service and treating the many cases of "shell shock" captured the public imagination. The National Committee gained recognition as well, for it was the group that organized the army's psychiatric services. Buoyed by their successes during the war and anxious to use their techniques on all kinds of conduct disorders, psychiatrists began to move into new fields—education, business, and social work, among others—once peace returned.

Psychiatrists, however, were in no position to treat all of America's behavior problems. Their numbers were small, their training spotty, and their view of the situation myopic. Clinical psychologists, although suffering from the same difficulties, understandably objected to psychiatry's new pretensions. The psychiatrist, complained Robert S. Woodworth of Columbia, had been "staking out, on paper, an exclusive claim to a large unoccupied domain, and insisting that the psychologist shall only work there in subordination to himself."[11] In 1920 the National Research Council held a conference on relations between psychologists and psychiatrists which drew representatives from the major organizations in both fields. The meeting took on a combative air, in which neither side was prepared to compromise. Indeed, the participants could not even agree on how to define terms like "mental disease," "clinic," "measurement," "psychiatry," and "clinical psychology." The prospects for mutually satisfying cooperation thus remained dim.

An incident in Missouri shows how clinical psychologists and psychiatrists could work at cross-purposes. J. E. Wallace Wallin, a clinical psychologist in St. Louis, had labored for several years to establish a state Bureau for Mental Defectives. As set forth in the proposed legislation that he managed to have drafted, the bureau was to classify the mentally deficient who were in state institutions, provide expert witnesses on mental defect, and collect data on mental deficiency in Missouri. By 1920 Wallin had gathered the appropriate endorsements for the proposal and was expecting its passage. He believed he was on the verge of establishing by law the supremacy of clinical psychology in one of its disputed borderlands with psychiatry.

Then a representative of the National Committee for Mental Hygiene came on the scene. He had been taking a survey of mental deficiency in Missouri, and upon learning of the proposed bureau, he attacked it on the grounds that he would not be directed by a psychiatrist. He further objected to divorcing the treatment of the feeble-minded from that of the insane. Wallin never attempted to work out a compromise with the National Committee, nor was he able to arrange a public debate on the issues. Using what Wallin later called "stealthy underground tactics," the National Committee's representative successfully lobbied against the bill, which died before reaching the floor of the state senate. Thus Missouri got no bureau at all.[12] The issues in dispute were probably too bound up in the professional identities of clinical psychologists and psychiatrists to have permitted a negotiated settlement.

The mental hygiene movement took a significant step (and clinical psychology lost a crucial round) in 1921 when the National Committee set up its first child guidance clinic. Financed by the Commonwealth Fund, it was part of a national program of demonstration clinics designed to attack mental problems during the formative years of childhood. After some initial difficulties the establishment of child guidance clinics gained rapid public support. In 1932 the National Committee announced that over half of America's 50 largest cities had clinics operating full time and that the national total, including part-time facilities, had reached 232. The Commonwealth Fund had hoped originally to use the clinics in the prevention of delinquency, but the twenties witnessed a shift of emphasis toward problems of maladjustment in home and school. This trend marked a further encroachment into the realm of the psychologists.

Psychiatrists did not intend to eliminate psychologists entirely from clinical work. On the contrary, the psychologist was a necessary member of the clinical "team." The concept of therapeutic teamwork, developed by William Healy in his treatment of delinquents, grew from the belief that every case required a three-pronged approach. Ideally, the team captain, the psychiatrist, provided psychotherapeutic treatment; the clinical psychologist administered tests; and the social workers developed case histories. In practice, however, the duties of the psychiatrist and social worker began to merge. It became increasingly difficult to distinguish between treatment and case history, in part because psychoanalytic psychiatry had an intrinsically historical method and in part because social work was adopting psychiatric theory as the conceptual foundation for its own professional aspirations. Psychology, however, remained distinct, and some of its practitioners felt themselves becoming alienated from the basic work of the clinic.

Most clinical psychologists did have some opportunity to treat patients in the course of their work. Their "teammates" usually granted them primacy in dealing with educational problems, so their involvement in treatment depended to some extent on how frequently a clinic accepted such cases. Otherwise, there were no general rules: a psychologist's use in therapy might be determined by his past experience and training, his ability to get along with patients, or his success in winning the confidence of the supervising psychiatrist. A survey in 1932 found that although 80 percent of clinical psychologists spent some of their time on remedial teaching, vocational guidance, or psychotherapy, testing remained their primary duty. Most clinical psychologists accepted their role as appropriate to their scientific training and interests. Those who sought greater contact with patients, however, became dissatisfied with the limited opportunities for therapy.

Although the seeds of conflict had been planted, psychiatrists and clinical psychologists were by no means in mortal combat during the twenties. Both groups worked almost entirely in institutional settings, so they did not compete for clients. Private practice, which had begun in psychoanalytic psychiatry, was virtually unknown in clinical psychology. In fact, of the psychologists in the APA's Clinical Section in 1930, only two listed themselves as private consultants.

In addition, psychiatrists themselves were not united, because their field was still largely concerned with the treatment of psychotic patients in mental institutions. Most psychiatrists sought neurological explanations of aberrant behavior. They often held stronger doubts about the scientific basis of psychoanalysis than about that of psychological testing. In response, those psychiatrists working on "clinical teams" sought allies among their coworkers. The Orthopsychiatric Association, created in 1930, formalized the alliance in a national organization of psychiatrists, social workers, and clinical psychologists.

A poll of veteran clinical psychologists taken in 1978 provides more data on their relationship with psychiatrists in the twenties. Asked if they believed that psychiatrists tried to devise policies to restrict the professional development of clinical psychology during the period, 37 percent said yes. Fewer, however, were personally affected. Only 13 percent believed that they had experienced such restrictions in their own careers during the period.[13]

This lack of personal involvement in professional conflict may have weakened organizational efforts in the twenties. Most clinical psychologists simply had no reason to band together. In psychiatric clinics, where about half of the full-time clinicians worked, generally good relations prevailed among staff members. Perhaps partly for this reason, the APA drew only about one-fifth of the country's clinical psychologists into the association.

That something like 80 percent of clinical psychologists did not join the APA also indicated a deep division between academic and clinical psychology. A major part of the problem lay in the attitudes of the professors. "Clinical psychology," wrote Henry H. Goddard, "has so far proved of interest to only a very small percentage of the students and teachers of psychology and what is still more to the point, very few of those who are interested in clinical psychology take it seriously."[14] This meant that few adequate training programs existed and that many promising students were not encouraged to enter the field. Academic psychologists often saw clinical psychology as menial work done in a subservient role. It was, observed John J. B. Morgan of Northwestern University, "not the work for a man."[15]

Francis N. Maxfield of Ohio State University, using similar terms to designate the low status of clinical psychologists, agreed that there was "little place in clinical psychology for young men at the present time."[16] Apparently, however, clinical work remained suitable for young women. Statistics confirmed that clinical psychology was in fact women's work. A survey in 1932 revealed that 63 percent of all America's clinical psychologists were women. The numerical preponderance of women in applied work had its greatest impact in the clinical field. One may speculate on the extent to which academic psychologists did not take clinical psychology seriously because they did not take women seriously. In any case, academicians were doing little to turn clinical psychology into "man's work."

Moreover, clinical psychologists with academic connections had not committed themselves to clinical work. J. E. Wallace Wallin believed this might be a major reason why psychiatrists had been successful in their struggles with psychologists. "The psychologists," he observed, ". . . were less vociferous and aggressive than psychiatrists, possibly because they were less dependent for their living upon professional practice than were the psychiatrists: they could continue in, or return to, the academic field of teaching and research."[17] Into this category fell many of the most prestigious names in clinical psychology: developers of tests, authors of textbooks, and workers in psychological organizations. In a sense then, the leading clinical psychologists did not strongly identify themselves with the field.

By the early thirties it had become clear that psychologists were failing even to achieve equality in clinical work. Psychiatrists, relying on their prestige as doctors and benefiting from the mental hygiene movement, had gone a long way in convincing the public that behavioral peculiarities were mental illnesses that needed treatment by physicians. In 1930 Wallin angrily told his colleagues that it was time to take decisive action or surrender. Rhetorically asking, "Shall We Continue to Train Clinical Psychologists for Second-String Jobs?" he declared that either psychologists must tell students interested in clinical work to become doctors or they must organize to "neutralize inimical propaganda," win popular support, and secure favorable legislation.[18] The article took as its premise the undeniable fact that psychological organizations had been doing little since the war to advance professional goals. Developments within the APA clearly show why achievements had been few.

The postwar era opened on a hopeful note for applied psychologists when the APA granted them a significant concession in 1919. Faced with the prospect that a new national organization, the American Association of Clinical Psychologists, might emerge to challenge it, the APA created its Clinical Section to deal with professional issues. Membership in the section was limited to APA members with doctorates and a research interest in testing or clinical work. Others in the APA were leery of the new group, which seemed to be operating outside traditional scientific and scholarly limits, and they wanted it to move very slowly and carefully. Many applied psychologists, however, looked on the formation of the Clinical Section as the first of several steps that would lead to a deep involvement by the APA in professional issues. The section established, its members turned next to the question of certification.

In 1919 the APA set up its Standing Committee on the Certification of Consulting Psychologists, and in 1921 the certification committee proposed a two-part plan to have the association devise and maintain national standards. The first part, which won APA approval, created within the association a section (later a division) of consulting psychologists. Membership in the new group, which was open only to those who were already in the Clinical Section, constituted certification by the APA that a member was competent to make diagnoses and give treatment of a psychological nature. The association issued a document that looked something like a high school diploma to each member of the consulting section. The certificate bore the signature of the president of the APA and stated that the association had found the holder to be "by training and experience qualified to advise psychologically in the adjustments of individuals. . . ."[19]

This type of certification, while an unprecedented action for the association, amounted to little beyond saying that APA members were psychologists. Any member who wanted a certificate and had the $35 fee for its issuance could obtain it. The APA refused to go beyond this in 1921, as seen by its reaction to the second half of the certification committee's proposal. The committee recommended that the association establish licentiates in mental measurement for nonmembers. It was a difficult prospect at best. The plan required the APA first to evaluate the education and experience of many people who had no scholarly interests or pretensions and then to back up the judgment with its hard-won and still tenuous scientific prestige. In this way the APA was directly to attack the incompetents and the charlatans who had arisen in such great numbers after the war. The plan held obvious risks, and the association rejected it.

In 1922 the certification committee proposed another scheme to broaden the APA's certification activities. It recommended that the association establish sections of industrial and educational psychology, membership in which would signify competence to practice in these fields. The APA responded by setting up committees to look into the prospects of the new sections. They found that industrial psychologists were generally but unenthusiastically favorable to a special section and educational psychologists had mixed reactions to the idea. Neither group was about to stage a rebellion like that of the clinical psychologists in 1917, and the association saw no pressing need to institute the new sections. The certification committee's proposal died without final action ever being taken on it. The APA's certification program thus remained limited and incomplete.

In 1923 the association received the first report of its Standing Committee on the Relation of Psychology to the Public Welfare. The committee had been set up a year before to represent the APA in efforts to correlate training in psychology with that in medicine and hygiene, to study the use of psychological testing in education, and to define the legal status of psychologists. It looked to many as if the association were going to use the committee to tackle some crucial professional issues. Perhaps with other committee members it might have done just that. The committee as constituted, however, decided to assume a passive role. It reported for three consecutive years that it had taken no action on any matter. In 1925 the APA dissolved the committee on the committee's own request. A potential move toward professionalism had come to nothing.

While the APA was taking only faltering steps on professional issues, an event occurred that promised to increase the influence of applied psychologists within the association. In 1923 the APA decided to develop an associate status for psychologists who could not meet the scholarly requirements of regular membership. Ironically the need for expanding the ranks of the organization grew out of two developments in academic psychology.

First, graduate departments were turning out Ph.D.s faster than the APA could absorb them. Because the days were ending when all research found its way into print, a lack of publications no longer necessarily indicated a deficiency in scholarly interest. By demanding published research beyond the dissertation the association was becoming unrepresentative of a growing part of academic psychology. Second, the APA had decided to get into the publication business by starting a journal of abstracts and buying the Psychological Review Company. The association, while economically sound, was in no position to assume added financial burdens without an increase in income. Associates, through their dues, could help to fill the APA's coffers.

In 1924 the APA created the grade of associate for persons in three classes: full-time professional workers in psychology, recipients of doctorates from recognized psychology departments, and eminent scholars or practitioners in related fields. Their participation in the organization was limited. Associates were not allowed to hold office in the APA, vote in elections, or even speak at business meetings. They could, however, attend the annual convention, present papers, and mingle with their betters. In the APA *Year Book* only an "(A)" before their names distinguished them from full members. The committee that devised the new status reminded the APA that the number of associates might soon equal the number of members. The prediction proved accurate. The APA admitted its first associates in 1925; by 1929 associates already outnumbered full members.

Applied psychologists—practitioners rather than scholars—now had the opportunity to join the APA. If the association met them with open palms more often than open arms, it nevertheless gave them a national organization for the first time. The APA was by no means theirs: the 1930 *Year Book* showed that the percentage of nonacademic psychologists among associates was only a bit higher than among full members. Since many practitioners who were eligible for associate status decided not to join the APA, the association did not contain everyone who was performing psychological work in America, but it at least came close to including all who identified themselves as psychologists.

Some applied psychologists may have remained outside the association, awaiting its response to professional issues. If so, they waited in vain. The creation of the associate grade did not signal an expansion in the certification program. In 1925 the certification committee made a detailed report on standards that could be used for certification. The APA Executive Council accepted the report but refused to publish it. At the annual business meeting a motion lost which would have permitted the report to be privately printed and distributed. "It is important to note," one council member later observed, "that this report, which for the first time contained detailed qualifications for consulting psychologists was completely pigeon-holed and was not adopted for the instruction and guidance of the committee."[20]

In 1926 came a hint of scandal. The certification committee reported that a psychologist (presumably a male certificate-holder) was having sexual relations with one of his clients. The committee's executive officer, Frederic Lyman Wells, urged the APA Executive Council to repudiate such activity, but it refused to do so. The "prevailing sentiment in the Association," Wells believed, had rendered the committee helpless in a case of profound significance for the professionalization of psychology. Unless the APA was prepared to regulate members' conduct, Wells argued, "professional standards comparable to those of law or medicine, cannot be established under the American Psychological Association. . . ." He was understandably discouraged about the chances of moving the APA in this direction.[21]

The certification committee in its published report for 1926 requested that the APA either clearly state that the association was not responsible for members' actions or set up a procedure to combat unprofessional conduct. The committee doubted, however, that the APA, as a group with scientific objectives, had the stamina to prevail over a member who was fighting to save his career. As a result, the committee concluded, the case for a professional organization outside the APA grew stronger. Members of the Clinical Section voiced similar beliefs at their 1926 meeting. They spoke of splitting the Clinical Section from the APA and of forming a new organization under which certification could make more progress. They did not take action on their ideas, however.

Meanwhile the APA appointed a new committee to evaluate the current certification scheme and to survey association members about their views on certification. While those in charge of certification were raising professional issues, they had been doing very little certifying. In 1927 only twenty-five psychologists held certificates. The chairman of the new committee had an explanation for this: "The present conditions of certification," she stated, "require so high a standard that those persons who can meet it are so well established that they need no certification."[22] Psychologists who favored certification had, of course, offered several ways to make it more comprehensive and more effective: the licensing of practitioners outside the APA, the inclusion of other applied psychologists besides clinicians, the development and enforcement of professional standards. The new committee found another solution, however, which was shortly to be adopted by the APA Council.

At the annual business meeting in 1927 the APA Executive Council, which included members of the Clinical Section, unanimously recommended that the division of consulting psychologists be abolished, that certificate holders be refunded their $35 issuance fee, and that the Clinical Section be prohibited from certifying its members. These proposals naturally provoked much discussion, but the council clearly had the votes to pass them. A motion lost that would have put the APA on record in favor of certifying its members in some manner. Another motion that the association state that it desired to certify psychologists outside the APA also failed. Then the business meeting passed the council's recommendations by a large majority. The APA thus ended its certification program.

The APA's action at the 1927 meeting cast a pall over the Clinical Section. The section did not meet in 1928; its chairman polled its members and found interest and enthusiasm for the section to have declined considerably. The association remained solidly in the hands of the academicians, who were unhappy at the prospect that their organization might stray from its scholarly path. They had allowed but never actually supported the APA's hesitant actions on professional issues. It was doubtful, commented a former APA secretary, that "the question of the control of applied or professional work in psychology will be attempted by the Association again for some time to come." Then he added what Clinical Section members knew all too well: "After all the Association is a scientific rather than a professional body."[23]

Thus, applied psychologists had only partial success in capitalizing on the immense popularity of their discipline in the period between war and depression. Their numbers increased dramatically, but in part because of expanded interest in academic psychology a large proportion of the new psychologists remained on college campuses. Those who did venture out into the world found their roles poorly defined. Psychological testing took hold firmly in schools and more tenuously in industry, yet in an attempt to make testing popular psychologists had not insisted on skillful testers. As a result many quasi-psychological jobs—guidance counseling in education or personnel work in business, for example—were lost to professional psychology. Had the demand for psychological service arisen less quickly, perhaps psychologists would have had the time to develop these jobs into branches of their own discipline.

As it was, clinical work offered the psychologists the best opportunity to use their tools and techniques. Unfortunately for them, however, Freudianism, the psychological theory that enjoyed the most popular acclaim after World War 1, was quickly expropriated by psychiatrists. Clinical psychologists often found themselves operating in the reflected light of psychiatry rather than shining on their own. Nor did they receive much help from their academic colleagues. The academicians, while eagerly exploiting the growth of psychology on campus, saw in its popularity in the outer world more of a threat than an opportunity. Generally, they kept a scholarly reserve and hoped thus to maintain their shaky status as scientists.

Nevertheless the period witnessed important advances in the professionalization of applied psychology. The ranks of practicing psychologists increased to the point that an effective national organization became a realistic possibility. While there remained the problem of psychologists who held divided allegiance between academics and practice, a strong professional consciousness was growing among some applied psychologists. They had a clear idea of what professional status was and a strong urge to attain it. They discovered most painfully that certification by the APA was not a workable method of achieving their ends. An increasing number of psychologists, academicians as well as practitioners, were coming to believe that only an organization outside the APA could press forward effectively on professional issues. Progress seemed likely to be slow. No psychologist in 1930 could have imagined the changes in applied psychology that depression and war would bring.

4

PSYCHOLOGISTS AND THE DEPRESSION

In January 1934 the *New York Times* noticed that psychologists had kept strangely silent about the economic difficulties that gripped the nation. "Every other trade and profession has gone on record," the *Times* observed, but psychologists, who had previously dispensed advice so freely, now proposed no solutions. Although politicians saw the psychological aspects of social problems—President Roosevelt, for example, said that America's great task was banishing fear—they were apparently getting their psychological prescriptions secondhand. "Where," the *Times* wondered, "are the psychologists themselves, with their complexes and their reflexes?"[1]

Writing in the *Atlantic Monthly,* Grace Adams offered an explanation for the psychologists' silence. Psychology, she declared, had been a fraud from the beginning. Psychologists fooled everyone into looking for the psychological roots of social issues, but the coming of the depression exposed the vacuousness of their approach.

One might imagine that the psychologists would have taken full advantage of [the depression, she jeered]; that the clinicians would have started to compile the longest and most tedious case history of their careers; that the professors would have rushed their latest theories into print; that the technicians of the laboratories would have set up the most stupendous reaction experiment of all time; . . . and that the lowliest member of the psychologists' guild would have made at least six suggestions for turning our defeatist mental attitude back once more to rosy optimism.

That psychologists had done none of these things Adams took as a sign of psychology's imminent demise.[2]

The psychologists' apparent silence may be explained in other ways. Many psychologists had felt uncomfortable during the twenties in the roles of magician and mind reader. Viewing themselves primarily as scholars, they may have been quite content to return to their research and watch the economists and other social scientists try to solve America's problems. Other psychologists were giving advice as usual but found their audience shrinking. The people who looked inward to discover the source of their troubles might still embrace psychology, but a growing number became disenchanted with adjustment and believed that only social change could remedy their misfortunes. So psychologists relinquished their place in the public consciousness, although many may have hoped that they would yet hear an urgent call for their services.

It bothered some psychologists when the New Deal failed to summon them. In the campaign to banish fear, for example, psychologists might well believe that they had as much to offer as anyone else. Some of Watson's most famous experiments, in fact, had been on just this topic. But President Roosevelt did not include psychologists among his advisors, and no one in the national administration seemed to notice that they were missing. When the President established the Science Advisory Board in 1934, he found no reason to put a psychologist on the panel. Thus Harold E. Burtt of Ohio State was only engaging in happy fantasy when he voiced the hope "that ere long psychologists may sit around the council table in high places."[3]

Nor did the government feel compelled to consult psychologists about specific laws that had psychological ramifications. "By way of example," Walter Van Dyke Bingham asked his fellow industrial psychologists in 1937, "when the social security law was framed, were the unemployment-insurance and old-age-pension provisions drafted after adequate investigation regarding the effects of such measures on workers' initiative, independence, and habits of thrift?"[4] Bingham could have asked this sort of rhetorical question just as easily about any other piece of New Deal legislation. He and his colleagues were anxious to be of service to the country, and they believed that they could make an important contribution. Unfortunately, the psychological research Bingham envisioned would have been prolonged and extensive, would have taxed the limits of the psychologists' competence, and would have convinced very few people whatever its result.

It soon became clear that the depression was having more effect on the psychologists than they were having on it. The academic job market felt the squeeze in the early thirties. A survey by a committee of the APA revealed that 100 new doctoral recipients in 1932 were competing for only

32 newly created positions. The situation in 1933 promised to be even grimmer: 129 new Ph.D.s in psychology and 46 fewer jobs than the year before. The chances of finding a position in higher education with only a master's degree virtually disappeared. In 1932 and 1933, the survey showed, American psychology departments would produce 736 graduates at the master's level but no new academic jobs for them at all. Higher education had traditionally absorbed most of the Ph.D.s and some of the M.A.s in psychology; figures for the early thirties indicated that this tradition would soon be broken.

The shriveling of the academic marketplace affected psychology departments throughout the country. One can easily imagine long-faced graduate students cheerlessly pursuing their studies with small chance of a scholarly career and startled professors discovering that they could no longer find academic positions for their youthful charges. Graduate departments, moreover, faced the obvious threat of stagnation or decline. In 1929 psychology, with 5 percent of all American Ph.D.s, held a respectable piece of the academic pie. But psychologists could hardly expect to maintain graduate enrollments if no jobs existed for new Ph.D.s. In fact, the proportion of doctorates in psychology did not reach the 1929 level again for twenty years.

Psychologists came to realize that they could not maintain their academic standing without an expansion in the applied fields of psychology. The thirties witnessed a variety of schemes to put unemployed psychologists to work. In 1932 the *Psychological Exchange*, a new journal devoted to professional issues, suggested that state and federal governments cooperate to found civic institutes of psychology throughout the country. These institutions, which were supposed to become self-supporting, would provide therapy and guidance to the public and carry out all kinds of psychological research. J. E. Wallace Wallin proposed to both the Hoover and Roosevelt administrations that the government organize a "morale department." This agency, designed to combat psychological maladjustments arising from the depression, was to be staffed by teachers and social workers who had been trained by psychologists. After the arrival of the New Deal the Psychologists League of New York City drafted a proposal for a national bureau of consulting psychologists. The bureau through its regional units would provide psychological services to schools, settlement houses, courts, police departments, and other social agencies. These schemes would have made the government responsible in some degree for the successful adjustment of individuals. Not even the New Deal was prepared to go that far, and the proposals aroused no noticeable interest among government officials.[5]

Another way to create new jobs was to expand present services. Percival

M. Symonds of Teachers College at Columbia University had this in mind when he announced that "every school should have a psychologist." Symonds figured that one psychologist for every five hundred pupils would provide adequate service. It would also have put all of America's unemployed psychologists to work. The proposal met resistance from some educators who had found psychologists poorly trained to meet the wide range of school problems. Symonds, however, believed that much of this objection rested on a confusion between true psychologists and mere testers.[6] In any case, the proposal and the reaction to it raised the issues of training, standards, and definitions. If psychologists were to place more of their number in applied jobs, they would have to turn their attention to professional issues.

Albert T. Poffenberger's presidential address to the APA in 1935, entitled "Psychology and Life," gave clear proof that professional problems were penetrating the consciousness of academic psychology. Poffenberger wondered if the association did not "draw too sharp a distinction between the professional and the professorial," thereby hiding the wisdom of its members in scholarly journals and leaving the popular mind open to frauds and amateurs. He suggested that little was being done "to give our well trained but unemployed psychologists an even chance with those who are both untrained and unscrupulous." The public needed some criteria to use in picking out the genuine psychologists. "The label 'psychologist,' " Poffenberger declared, "must eventually come to stand for something in the way of uniformity and stability of the product, both for the good of the public and for the psychologist himself." And to the APA, the only group "sufficiently disinterested, sufficiently powerful and sufficiently representative of the country as a whole," fell the responsibility of defining terms and setting standards.

Poffenberger continued by citing other reasons why the APA should take a greater interest in applied psychology. He pointed out that a third of its total membership did not list an academic affiliation in the 1935 *Year Book.* "With the predicted limitation of growth within our academic institutions during the next decade," he observed, "this proportion of the non-academic psychologist is certain to increase." At the same time unemployment was high and growing "at an alarming rate." Rather than cut back graduate enrollments, as some schools had done, Poffenberger recommended an extension of psychological service. The APA could not fill the needs of its members and maintain its prestige if it dodged the problems of unemployment and the related professional issues.

In conclusion Poffenberger offered a six-point program that would recognize psychology as an applied as well as a pure science and would broaden psychology's effect on the community. The APA, he urged, should define *"homo psychologicus"* and propose standards of training both for psychologists in general and for those in the major applied fields. It should survey nonacademic jobs that could "provide employment for the growing army of psychologists." Finally, the APA should find ways to protect the public against both the claims of the charlatan and the deliberate misrepresentations of genuine psychologists. Poffenberger believed these "drastic proposals" were "in the spirit of the times," and he hoped "a fair minority" of the association would receive them sympathetically.[7]

Poffenberger's program contained no startling innovations. The development of uniform training for applied jobs and the banishment of frauds from the public marketplace had concerned some psychologists for twenty years. Helping people to find work was hardly a novel idea in 1935. Poffenberger, nevertheless, feared a negative reaction because he proposed that despite its scholarly aspirations the APA itself undertake these activities. By the 1930s few psychologists doubted that some group ought to take up professional problems; the question was whether Poffenberger's colleagues would agree that applied and academic psychology were so intertwined that one organization must handle them both.

In fact, the APA did not pursue a consistent policy in the thirties. Sometimes it seemed to be on the verge of deep involvement in professional issues; at other times it sloughed off these responsibilities on other organizations. Meanwhile academically trained psychologists established new groups that proposed to extend the range of psychological practice.

In 1933 the APA assigned several new tasks to the committee that had just reported on the gloomy job market. The committee, among other things, was to discover what made up the current standards of training for applied work and to consider how graduate programs could be changed to emphasize practical applications of psychological study. This broad mandate might have led to a redefinition of the whole nature of psychology. But the committee, finding its duties hopelessly vague, never even managed to get started. One member quit, branding the operation futile, and Poffenberger, the chairman, reported that "to tamper too much with the laws of supply and demand even in psychology may be a precarious business. . . ." Having failed to find any simple and beneficial way to alter the status quo, the committee was dissolved at its own request in 1934.[8]

Unfortunately, unemployment did not disappear so easily. In May 1935 a group of young psychologists met in Chicago to discuss the situation. Seeing little chance for academic positions, they requested that the APA appoint a committee to approach the federal government about using relief funds to employ psychologists on worthwhile projects. In addition, they began a nationwide petition campaign designed to show support for such an initiative by the association. In three months the campaign generated some three hundred signatures; most were from APA members and associates, although many graduate students also signed. Never before had psychologists tried to petition the APA for a redress of grievances. Their decision to do so in the spring of 1935 indicated that unemployment was having a greater impact on psychologists than any previous issue, professional or academic.

A year and a half before, the association's secretary and chief executive officer, Donald G. Paterson, had denied that the APA had a responsibility to find government jobs for psychologists. That was the concern, he then believed, of the National Research Council's Division of Anthropology and Psychology.[9] Impressed perhaps by the unprecedented flood of signatures, Paterson changed his mind in June 1935. He assured the petitioners that the APA's executive council would consider the problem of unemployment at its annual meeting in September and would "do everything possible to meet the needs of the situation."[10] What turned out to be possible was the establishment of two new committees.

The Committee on the Social Utilization of Unemployed Psychologists, formed in 1935 with Poffenberger as chairman, assumed responsibility for compiling the names and qualifications of psychologists who were out of work and for finding ways to obtain jobs for them on projects of social value. The committee began in September by polling the entire APA membership for information about psychologists who were either unemployed or on relief. By October it had found 180 such psychologists, of whom Poffenberger estimated 150 were employable. He believed this number too small for a special government project. "There is simply no use," he argued, "in trying to make a big blast about help for the unemployed psychologists of the nation when we can point to only 150 of them."[11]

Having abandoned grand schemes, Poffenberger's committee turned itself into an employment bureau. Corresponding with public and private agencies across the country, it tried to find suitable jobs for specific individuals. After a year of this effort, however, the committee reported little sense of success: it may have helped some people, but it had no reliable way to know for sure. In New York City, where the job crisis was most acute, the committee worked with local groups to try to find WPA positions for psychologists. It discovered that no one on its jobless list was sufficiently destitute to be eligible for the WPA. In addition, Poffenberger believed that jobs in the WPA would give little opportunity for steady and useful psychological work. Concluding with a plea that the APA assume greater interest in preparing psychologists for work in applied fields, the committee asked in 1936 to be discharged.

The association could have continued the committee, appointing different members and then perhaps expanding its operations into a genuinely effective employment agency. However, with grassroots pressure subsiding the APA removed itself from the task of finding jobs for the unemployed and dissolved the committee. Despite a sincere effort, Poffenberger and other committee members had accomplished little. Some psychologists might justifiably be dissatisfied, but the fault lay as much with the association as the committee.

In 1935 the APA also created the Committee on Psychology and the Public Service. Its chairman, L. J. O'Rourke, was Director of Research in Personnel Administration of the U.S. Civil Service Commission and the highest ranking APA member in the federal bureaucracy. O'Rourke's committee assumed the task of synchronizing college programs in psychology with civil service requirements, hoping finally to place more people with psychological training in government jobs. During the next few years the committee had some success in seeing that job specifications were rewritten so that psychology courses became acceptable preparation for certain positions. The committee reported no luck, however, in persuading psychology departments to revise their curricula in order to bring their programs in line with civil service requirements.

The work of O'Rourke's committee represented another important step away from the APA's traditional orientation toward research. Perhaps it would have received more support within the association if it had promoted the utilization of psychologists in specifically psychological jobs rather than simply trying to give psychologists a chance to compete for existing positions. In any case, APA members did begin trickling into government service during the thirties. Their numbers, however, remained small—fewer than fifty in 1937, for example—and their efforts were sprinkled among a great variety of agencies and departments.

Judged by ordinary criteria of effectiveness, the APA's efforts on employment and other professional issues came to very little. The leaders of the association, motivated by a sense of moral obligation rather than economic interest, established committees that had breathtaking responsibilities but small chances for success. Few academic psychologists wanted to experiment with their graduate programs, deemphasize research, or bring their departments under any kind of centralized control. Nevertheless, considered against what the organization had been willing to do in the past, the APA's involvement during the depression in matters outside the realm of pure scholarship marked an unprecedented assumption of professional responsibility.

As the depression wore on, some psychologists began to believe that politics might emerge as a possible new field of application. Because no one had voiced a demand for their services in solving social problems and because their colleagues feared losing the veneer of scientific objectivity, these psychologists faced a difficult time in getting themselves established.

The initiators of the new group had some cause for optimism, because they were largely the same ones who had organized the impressive petition campaign in 1935. They belonged to a left-wing political organization called New America, which was not affiliated with the Communist party but which espoused a sufficiently radical ideology to make more conservative psychologists a bit skittish.

In the spring of 1936 an organizing committee circulated to the entire membership of the APA a proposal for the foundation of the new society. Its purposes were to be threefold: to promote research on social issues, to prepare and publish findings on the psychological impacts of the depression, and to encourage psychologists to become involved as psychologists in contemporary problems. The plan received an excellent response, and prospects for the emergence of the new group looked bright.

Since the new society was to be composed primarily of academicians, the question of its relationship with the APA arose immediately. Its founders desired to use the facilities and capitalize on the prestige of the older association. They doubted, however, that the APA would allow itself to become involved in political activities. I. Krechevsky (David Krech), the secretary of the organizing committee, had already heard complaints that he was trying to establish a left-wing propaganda group within the association. Krechevsky feared that substantial opposition within the APA would prevent a close association of the two groups.

The APA, however, had been devising a scheme to keep all psychological interest groups close at hand. The plan had originated in 1935 when a group of psychologists had formed the Psychometric Society, an organization devoted to the use of mathematics in psychology. Its leaders had desired to maintain friendly relations with the APA, but they had opposed the idea of becoming a mere section of the association. The APA Council, having decided not to set up an opposing organization, had opted instead for a policy of close cooperation with the new group. Soon thereafter the Psychometric Society had become the APA's first affiliated organization.

The APA Council had not intended that affiliation should apply to the Psychometric Society alone, however. Even while the psychologists interested in social issues were organizing themselves, the council was establishing conditions under which other organizations might become affiliates. Although the APA would remain the largest, wealthiest, and most prestigious psychological group, paternalistic cooperation rather than dominance was to be the goal. "Even if we are no longer to have an empire," wrote one officer of the APA in 1935, "I hope we may maintain a commonwealth of nations."[12]

Working under this mandate, Paterson did not wish to see any national group of reputable psychologists, including those interested in social issues, operating outside the association's orbit. At the same time, he dared not compromise the APA's scientific reputation. Paterson opposed trading scholarly objectivity for political agitation, and he did not believe psychologists should speak on social issues in their role as psychologists. Hence he sought assurances from Krechevsky, agreeing to support the new group only if its sole object was research. Krechevsky quickly accepted the offer. "We are entering this project as scientists," he stated, "with but one aim—to foster research on problems of social significance in psychology." Apparently satisfied, Paterson promised to publicize the new group's organizational meeting and to raise no opposition to its eventual affiliation with the APA.[13]

In September 1936 the new organization established itself as the Society for the Psychological Study of Social Issues (SPSSI). Its membership, which soon exceeded three hundred, consisted almost entirely of academicians. Only members of the APA and other scholarly groups were permitted to join the SPSSI, further committing the new society to research. The bylaws of the organization did not encourage members in their capacity as psychologists to take stands on political issues. The SPSSI's first purpose was "to work effectively for both the immediate and ultimate freedom of psychology to do its utmost to make contemporary American society intelligible to its members," a goal presumably vague enough to satisfy both cloistered and activist psychologists.[14] The society also said it would promote and protect psychological research in economics and politics and would encourage applying the results of psychological investigations to social problems. The APA accepted the new organization as an affiliate in 1937.

The SPSSI organized its first research projects in 1937, forming committees to produce scholarly but readable volumes on the psychological aspects of industrial conflict and international warfare. It also set up a committee that studied and later recommended union membership for psychologists. Its contact with the general public remained limited, however, consisting mostly of a few statements on social issues. A week before Armistice Day in 1937 the SPSSI issued a news release explaining why war was not psychologically unavoidable. The *New York Times* handled the statement as a regular news item, and the Women's International League for Peace and Freedom later reprinted it in a separate leaflet. The SPSSI's later declarations—on popular character analysis and mental breakdowns in wartime—received less public attention, however. When in September 1938 SPSSI members heard their chairman tell them that psychology was destined to be used in resolving social problems, they had not yet found an effective method to become such instruments of fate.

In the spring of 1937 some members of the SPSSI helped to organize a group that had no scholarly pretensions—the Psychologists Committee of the Medical Bureau to Aid Spanish Democracy. The committee formed a small part of a larger effort to send medical personnel and supplies to the Spanish loyalists. At the APA convention the committee sponsored a talk and film on the situation in Spain. The presentation drew a capacity audience and raised some $1,200 for the Medical Bureau. The committee's efforts did not mean that psychology was joining the struggle against fascism; rather they indicated that many academic psychologists, like many Americans in other occupations, were genuinely worried about the collapse of democracy in Europe.

One group of American psychologists had no qualms about mixing psychology and politics. The Psychologists League of New York City emerged in the mid-thirties in direct response to the depression. Unlike most of the psychologists in the APA and SPSSI, few league members had established themselves in academic positions. Most of them had entered the job market after the flush days of the twenties. In addition, many league members were Jewish and thus victims of anti-Semitism within the universities. Of those who had found positions in applied fields, some were volunteering their services, hoping later to land paying jobs. The league also represented a less formally trained group of psychologists than did the national organization; only 20 percent of its two hundred members held doctorates at the end of 1937.

Many of the league's members had only a slim commitment to the status quo. They took the usefulness of psychology for granted and then posed broad questions about its meaning and function in American society. As its first purpose the league resolved to examine "the social roots and implications of psychology as a service, a science, and a profession." Beyond that its political intentions remained obscure. Although many of its activities placed the league squarely in the Popular Front, some of its members had little interest in left-wing politics. They found themselves attracted to other aspects of the group's program—the discussion of new therapeutic techniques, for example—and to the lively atmosphere of its meetings. The leaders of the league sought not ideological uniformity but agreement on general principles. In the spring of

1937 the league's *Journal* stated that the organization was "by no means committed to the exclusive use of any one politico-historical method of investigation." This declaration of neutrality, which would have made no sense in any other psychological publication, revealed the intense interest in politics and history that some league members possessed.[15]

The league urged its members to join New York's annual May Day parade in 1937. Arguing that the prosperity of science was tied to the welfare of "the great masses of our country," the league viewed the parade as an opportunity to demonstrate the solidarity of professional and working-class groups. Carrying placards that read "Adjustment Comes with Jobs!" and "Fascism Is the World's Worst Behavior Problem!" and shouting slogans like "Build More Clinics—You'll Need Less Prisons!" and "Down with Fascism, Up with Science," about seventy members marched in the league's contingent.[16] Such goings-on did not overly concern America's communist watchers. The league received only slight mention in the investigations of the House Un-American Activities Committee: in 1938 a witness claimed it was one of 640 groups involved in some way with the communist movement. More ominously perhaps, some members of the psychological establishment came to doubt the league's scholarly detachment.

The interests of many members of the league lay in its second stated purpose: to provide secure professional jobs for psychologists. Believing that a large, unfilled need existed for psychological services in public institutions, the league urged the federal government to employ more psychologists. The WPA, which received the organization's continuous attention, finally did open jobs for psychologists in some of its projects. Such positions were not only desirable in themselves, but they provided important examples of how psychology could be used in the government's social projects.

The league's persistent and often successful efforts on behalf of the unemployed goaded the older organizations into cooperative action. In his presidential address to the APA in 1935, Poffenberger specifically commended a league proposal for increased government jobs. "Why," he asked, "should an organization of the type of the Psychologists League have to be set up unless these very pressing problems were being neglected by existing agencies?"[17] Although the APA never endorsed the league's grand schemes, it did add its prestige to the league's efforts by agreeing in September 1936 to enter a joint committee on unemployment with the league.

Established practitioners may have been worried about the league's stand on professional issues. Writing for the league in 1935, Solomon Diamond argued that the call for higher standards was merely another way to limit the number of psychologists. This campaign would protect those already in the field, allow employers to pay apprentice wages to qualified psychologists, and insure prolonged graduate study. "This method of fitting the supply to the demand is definitely injurious to the interests of the profession as a whole," Diamond continued, "because the prospects for the progress of psychological science and for its increased social effectiveness are largely determined by the opportunities offered to young people entering the field."[18] In 1937 the league stated its approval of excluding unqualified practitioners, but it feared proposals that might eliminate psychologists who for financial reasons had not received the doctorate or the required experience. The proper way to combat charlatans, the league argued, was through the creation of new public service jobs for genuine psychologists.

Many applied psychologists viewed the league as a threat to professionalization. Horace B. English, for example, one of applied psychology's leading organizers, objected to trying to find jobs for practitioners who had not received their doctorates. Later English found other reasons to be wary of the league. He contended that it encouraged incompetents, was controlled by communists, and had too many unassimilated Jews among its members. Thus the league posed a distinct threat to the future that English envisioned for applied psychology.[19]

The league represented psychologists whose youth, financial condition, and often ethnic affiliation excluded them from the academic establishment. As the only important psychological group not controlled by academicians, the league brought a special urgency to professional issues. No other organization, for example, had an employment committee whose members themselves were looking for work. The league consistently sought the social roots of psychological problems, and it saw no point in adjusting individuals to a poorly functioning society. A product of the depression, the league was likely to endure as long as economic conditions remained grim and the antifascist alliance among its members continued unimpaired.

The depression also witnessed intensified organizational efforts among applied psychologists. Many practitioners believed that the acquisition of professional status would afford the surest protection against economic dislocations, and they saw the establishment of an effective national organization as the next crucial step on the road to professionalism. Organizing such a group promised to involve a long and complicated series of maneuvers and compromises, but if a national association emerged that would act energetically on professional issues, then the time and effort required for its establishment would be repaid many times over.

In the early thirties the APA's Clinical Section, which had been moribund for several years, experienced a distinct revitalization. At the 1930 meeting members of the section read papers, appointed committees, and displayed a general enthusiasm about their group. By December 1932 the size of the section had grown to 232—an increase of 70 percent in one year. In the early thirties the section considered taking a survey of American psychological clinics, setting up a job information center, determining the legal status of psychologists in several states, and standardizing the training and experience needed for clinical work. In addition, the group began reconsidering its nemesis of the twenties, certification. The Clinical Section seemed to be getting back into action.

While the Clinical Section was enjoying this resurgence, another organization, the Association of Consulting Psychologists (ACP), came on the scene. The group had originated in 1921 as a statewide organization in New York. It became the strongest of about a dozen state groups that took up professional issues during the twenties and thirties. Only one of these issues—licensing—could realistically be pursued at the state level, and that effort required more lobbying than applied psychologists could muster in any state during the two decades. The state organizations, which were generally limited to the northeast quarter of the country, were able, of course, to attack purely local issues and provide moral support to their members.

In 1930 the New York group reorganized under its new name and began to concern itself with national issues. The ACP's constitution listed the organization's objectives: mutual benefit to consulting psychologists in all fields of applied work, the education of the public about psychological services, and the stimulation of research in consulting psychology. The ACP's concerns were clearly professional rather than academic, and its activities included work on state licensing, standardized training, differentiating levels of competence, and other issues of interest to practitioners.

The ACP also took up a professional matter that had previously received little formal attention: an ethical code for psychologists. In 1933 the organization proposed some general rules for its members, violations of which could lead to expulsion. The code began with the twin premises that "the work of the practicing psychologist constitutes a profession" and "the first aim of a profession is the service it can render humanity." In relations with the public, ACP members were enjoined from making outlandish claims or advertising without restraint. They pledged to publicize malpractice and to serve in "any public movement of recognized social value" if their knowledge and training made it appropriate. The code stated that no information obtained by a psychologist could be used for his own benefit, nor could it be published without the consent of his client. Members of the ACP were urged to adopt the American Bar Association's position on fees: they were not to soak the rich, but they might exempt the poor from payment. Finally, the code provided for ethical behavior among colleagues—there was to be no public quarreling, for example, and no commissions for referrals.[20]

Proposing the code represented an important step in applied psychologists' attempts to regulate the conduct of their colleagues. If the code's provisions could be enforced, they would guarantee ethical behavior and help to reassure the public. The ACP intended that reputable psychologists would have little to fear from the code, but the charlatans might well find their careers in jeopardy. Unfortunately, because it applied only to ACP members, the code could not be effectively enforced. People calling themselves psychologists came under neither legal nor moral pressure to join the organization. The effectiveness of the code thus depended on the effectiveness of the ACP itself. If it could gain enough power and prestige, it might force all applied psychologists either to join its ranks or to leave the field completely. Members realized, however, that the ACP would not win such influence quickly or easily.

By 1935 the ACP had begun expanding its operations beyond New York to nearby areas. Meanwhile members seriously considered combining the ACP with other local groups to form a national federation. Although it tried to maintain friendly relations with the Clinical Section of the APA, the ACP found that its efforts to expand beyond state borders led to some conflict between the two groups. In November 1934 the secretary of the Clinical Section, Edward B. Greene, asked Donald G. Paterson, the secretary of the APA, if the ACP's activities could be curtailed. The split between academic and applied psychology was, Greene believed, "bad for both and in many ways a farce." The Clinical Section had been established to handle professional issues, he argued, and the ACP provided unwarranted competition with it.[21] Greene represented that segment of the APA that wanted the association to drop its scholarly reserve and embrace all psychological activity, academic and applied.

Paterson, on the other hand, was most reluctant to see the APA lose its scientific orientation. Recalling the fate of certification schemes of the twenties, he doubted that the association could ever give wholehearted support to the practitioners within its ranks. Paterson suggested to Greene that "the Association of Consulting Psychologists is a natural response to the repeated refusal of the A.P.A. to make attempts, in any sustained manner, to control applied or professional work in psychology." Since the APA was "not prepared to solve" professional problems, he did not find the ACP in competition with it. Indeed, Paterson supported the activities of the ACP "with a free conscience" even while serving as the APA's chief executive officer.[22]

Paterson then moved to end the dispute once and for all. He told the APA's Executive Council that the Clinical Section had been ineffective in pursuing professional goals and argued further that the APA's corporate charter limited the association to scientific activities. The Executive Council agreed unanimously that the APA and its Clinical Section must avoid professional issues. Council members cited the American Medical Association as a group that had turned itself into a trade union through growing involvement in nonscientific activities. The danger arose that scientists might one day be driven from the APA. The council welcomed the formation of the ACP in the hope that the new organization could develop into a high-class professional group whose operations must necessarily benefit psychology as a whole.

A further indication of the council's desire to paralyze the Clinical Section came when none of its members challenged Paterson's contention that the corporate charter prohibited professional activities. The charter stated that "the object of the society shall be to advance psychology as a science," a statement so vague that only people predisposed to Paterson's interpretation of it could have accepted his interpretation without question. Greene vigorously protested the council's decision, but to no avail. In August 1935 a legal opinion stated that "the advancement of professional standards," one of the section's goals, was a permissible activity under the charter. By that time, however, debate on the APA's policy had closed.

With little left to do but provide a forum for research, the Clinical Section lost its fundamental purpose. In March 1935 Greene received a suggestion that the section leave the APA and join the ACP; this sentiment was to grow steadily in the following months. Thus the APA's increased involvement in professional issues did not preclude crippling its own section for practitioners. The whole issue was not yet settled, and opponents of the council's policy could still hope that one day the Clinical Section would rise again.

With a formidable obstacle removed from its path, the ACP moved vigorously to establish itself as a national organization. In the spring of 1935 its newsletter reported a recent upsurge of activity that provided "evidence of a dynamic organization in which professional pride has its rightful place."[23] In April the ACP set up a committee to promote the development of a federation of state and regional organizations. The committee also received instructions to urge the Clinical Section to "amalgamate" with the new group. Assured it would encounter no objection from the larger association, the ACP scheduled an organizational meeting for the proposed new federation during the September convention of the APA. The meeting, which drew representatives from fourteen groups, produced a consensus on the desirability of some sort of federation. Several problems arose, however, that precluded immediate action: the groups possessed a variety of purposes, they had differing membership standards, and they were of unequal size and influence since the ACP was by far the most powerful. The representatives returned home with these issues unresolved, but another meeting was scheduled for the following May. The leaders of the ACP hoped in the interim to find a workable plan for a national association.

The APA, meanwhile, had entered its commonwealth-of-nations phase, and the ACP's leaders realized that their organization could benefit from the new policy. In March 1936 Edgar A. Doll, the chairman of the committee that was considering a national federation of applied groups, wrote Paterson that the ACP was contemplating affiliation with the APA. Doll argued that the two organizations, which represented "merely two aspects of the same thing," should remain in close cooperation. He pointed out that professional activity in applied fields would promote "the scientific and academic interests of psychology" which were the main concern of the APA. Paterson, who had promoted both the expansion of the ACP and the idea of affiliation, needed little convincing. He stated his hope that the ACP could "work out some sort of affiliation with the American Psychological Association so that all of the special interest groups in psychology can be kept together in a helpful manner."[24] In May 1936 Doll's committee recommended that the ACP affiliate with the APA.

The ACP held a meeting in September that drew seventy-five representatives from state and regional groups. A large committee was then formed to work out the details of a new national organization for applied psychology. The committee came eventually to contain twenty-nine members, including spokesmen for the main fields of psychological practice, officers of both the ACP and the Clinical Section, and a delegate from the Psychological Corporation. Despite its seeming diversity, the committee hardly represented applied psychologists as a whole. A close look at its composition would have given a strong indication of the kind of organization it was likely to construct.

Of the 29 committee members only 10 had pursued nonacademic careers; the rest were college professors first and practitioners second. Virtually all were well established in their jobs—as might be expected of a group containing only 4 people born in the twentieth century. They thus remained personally unaffected by the shriveled job market that posed such a crucial problem for younger psychologists. Committee members had a strong interest in research: 24 had passed the stiff scholarly requirements for full membership in the APA. The other 5 held associate status; no one outside the association was involved in organizing the new national group. Finally, although most full-time applied psychologists were women, 27 of the 29 committee members were men. The committee consisted mostly of middle-aged men with well settled careers in teaching and research. They were the sort of people who might be expected to establish an organization that demanded high academic standards for practitioners and moved cautiously in all its endeavors. The committee proposed first that the idea of a federation be scrapped altogether. Only individuals would hold membership in the new organization; groups could affiliate under a scheme similar to the one recently established by the APA. Although affiliates would contain more members than the national organization, they would have only a small voice in the managing of its affairs. The plan, however, did include a board of affiliates through which local groups might coordinate their activities. The committee took the arrangement that had worked so poorly in the APA— sections based on special interests—and made it the key organizing principle of the new association. Four semiautonomous sections were to represent the fields of clinical, business and industrial, consulting, and educational psychology. The committee kept distinctions between sections intentionally vague, hoping to entice applied psychologists with one label or another.

In August 1937 over two hundred applied psychologists from the APA and the ACP held a final organizational meeting. They quickly agreed that the new association should have individual members, affiliated societies, and four sections. Membership standards, however, drew spirited debate. The meeting finally decided to establish two classes of members, "fellows" and "associates." Fellows needed to have had four years of psychological practice or to have published important research in applied psychology. Associates needed only one year of experience. A doctorate was required for both classes, but in special cases two years of self-directed practice might be substituted for it. While the new organization placed less emphasis on scholarship than did the APA, a psychologist could still achieve the rank of fellow solely on the basis of his research.

In the next few days the other national organizations in applied psychology removed themselves from competition with the new group. A poll of the Clinical Section in 1937 had revealed that 70 percent of the members favored its disbandment in favor of an organization that would respond more completely to professional needs. Many of the remaining 30 percent wanted the section to change in ways prohibited by the APA council. As a result, on 1 September the Clinical Section voted to dissolve and turn its assets over to the new association. The ACP quickly followed suit. Its executive committee, acting on the instructions of the members at a special meeting, voted on 2 September to disband the organization.

After several years of intense maneuvering and compromise, applied psychologists at last had an independent national organization.

The ACP willed its professional magazine, the *Journal of Consulting Psychology,* to the new group. The journal had begun publication in January 1937. Its bimonthly issues included summaries of research, articles on psychological services, organizational reports, book reviews, and news items. But the journal did more than provide information. Its editors deliberately sought to build esprit de corps among applied psychologists by manufacturing heroes. Each issue opened with a picture of a famous psychologist who had made notable contributions to professional psychology. Later the first dozen of these portraits, which the journal considered suitable for framing, were packaged for separate sale. One of the primary purposes of the new publication, explained the chairman of the editorial board, was to further the "group solidarity" of psychologists in applied work.[25]

The new organization got under way in the year following the September 1937 meeting. After some discussion it chose a descriptive but inoffensive name, the American Association for Applied Psychology (AAAP). It set up committees on the training of psychologists, relations with the public and other professions, techniques of applied psychology, and other professional issues. It adopted a formal constitution that contained provisions much like those agreed upon in 1937. The constitution stated that fellows of the AAAP must be either "actively engaged in the application of psychology *as their primary profession*" or "directing programs concerned with direct application or research relating thereto."[26] The italics perhaps indicated some unwillingness to admit the fact that most AAAP members were academicians. One new provision diluted the influence of practitioners still further by permitting psychologists who were primarily only teachers of applied psychology to become associates. Membership grew quickly in the new organization's first year, passing four hundred by September 1938.

The AAAP faced several problems that were likely to persist for some time. Some members questioned whether the new organization could represent the great variety of specialities and localities within applied psychology. Andrew W. Brown, chairman of the AAAP Clinical Section, feared that Douglas Fryer and Horace B. English, the AAAP's first president and executive secretary respectively, were trying to centralize the operations of the organization. Believing that applied psychology would be better off if each section worked on its own, Brown proposed at the 1938 business meeting that the AAAP constitute itself as a federation of independent societies.[27] The proposition sparked a vigorous debate in which its opponents pointed to the confusion, duplication of effort, and professional fragmentation that would result from its passage. These arguments proved convincing, and the proposal was overwhelmingly defeated.

Almost no one in the AAAP would have disagreed with the proposition that other professional groups would judge the new association on how effectively it restricted membership to truly competent practitioners. The perennial question, however, was what constituted competence; it arose very clearly in the case of Henry Feinberg, a clinical psychologist with the Jewish Social Service Bureau in Detroit. Several years before, Feinberg had organized a group interested in clinical psychology within the National Conference of Social Work. His speakers and displays continued to arouse interest, but by 1938 he was hoping to pass the work to the AAAP. Although the new association was ready to follow up on Feinberg's efforts, it could not accept Feinberg himself.

The problem, English explained, was that Feinberg had only a bachelor's degree. Since the AAAP waived the doctoral requirement only for those with master's degrees, Feinberg would not be allowed to join the new association. English claimed that he opposed overly formalistic standards, yet he wondered if the public would place psychologists on the same level with doctors and lawyers if they did not have to meet "high formal requirements." Feinberg pointed out that many psychologists without advanced degrees had been doing good work in their communities for many years. They had received recognition from social agencies and had published articles on their research. Feinberg thought such people deserved some affiliation with the AAAP. English was sympathetic but unyielding.[28] The college professors who organized the new association were determined to maintain the academic standards that excluded many of psychology's practitioners.

The AAAP had yet to work out a coherent policy toward the APA. Some AAAP members wanted to detach themselves from the older organization and move out energetically on their own. The more influential psychologists within the AAAP, however, favored close cooperation between the two groups. Even before the new association had been organized, Fryer was looking forward to the time when it would have enough prestige to amalgamate with the APA. English agreed that the AAAP should not stray very far from the older association, and he believed that he and Fryer could keep the more independently minded members in line. As president and executive secretary they were, he reported, "in a position to influence policy very materially—though democracy and fairness set limits on what we should do."[29] In addition, some AAAP members had opposed leaving the APA all along. They were hoping for a quick reunification of applied and academic psychology.

After twenty years of effort applied psychologists had finally managed to establish a national organization. They realized that the AAAP represented an important step in the professionalization of psychology, but they knew it was only a step. Setting up standardized training programs, banishing the charlatans from the field, promulgating and enforcing an ethical code—these problems required solutions before the public would accept the psychologists' claim to exclusive competence in performing an important social service. It was by no means clear that the AAAP with its divisions and its exclusiveness would move quickly and decisively on these crucial questions.

Despite the outburst of organizational activity and the unprecedented interest in professional issues during the thirties, applied psychologists in 1938 still faced many of their perennial problems. As usual, clinicians experienced the most trouble. Psychiatrists continued to oppose therapeutic practice by psychologists. Medicine was completing its own professionalization and naturally objected to any kind of treatment that both physicians and nonphysicians would perform. A poll of clinical psychologists who practiced in the thirties found that 40 percent believed that psychiatrists as a group tried to restrict the development of clinical psychology.

The same poll revealed that only 13 percent felt restricted in their own careers by psychiatrists. The low figure did not indicate unalloyed harmony between the two groups, however. Some clinical psychologists did not encounter any obstructions. Anna S. Elonen, for example, recalled that psychiatrists at the University of Chicago Clinic permitted "me and my staff to grow in all possible ways." Samuel J. Beck, who practiced in Boston and Chicago, largely agreed. "They [psychiatrists] encouraged and helped me . . . they took unremitting interest in my findings. . . ." But Beck remembered other aspects of the story: "The psychiatrists always assumed that as a class they were above psychologists and did not feel any competition from us." Gertrude Hildreth, who worked in the Lincoln School of Columbia University's Teachers College, had a similar impression. The psychiatrists in New York "didn't so much try to restrict or restrain the psychologists as to ignore them and avoid giving any recognition except as subordinates in the field. . . ." Where the psychologists and psychiatrists performed the same duties, another problem often arose. Charles L. Vaughn, who practiced in the Psychopathic Clinic of the Detroit Recorder's Court, recalled that "a psychiatrist working next to a psychologist and doing the same thing would make two or three times as much money." And psychologists, of course, were then earning depression-era wages.

Many of those who responded to the poll believed that psychologists and psychiatrists simply had little opportunity for conflict. Some respondents, because of their jobs or their locations, seldom encountered psychiatrists. In addition, with so few of either group in private practice, competition for clients was virtually nonexistent. Perhaps Townsend Lodge, who practiced in Cleveland during the late thirties, best summed up the reason that psychologists did not feel professionally restricted. "Role differences," he recalled, "seemed sharper then. . . ."[30]

Meanwhile the charlatans and the popularizers maintained a large audience. For example, the April 1938 issue of one popular magazine, the *Modern Psychologist,* offered readers such articles as "Memory Magic," "Radio Waves of the Mind," "Faith Makes Them Whole," and "Get What You Want." The magazine also featured advertisements for many quasi-psychological goods and services: a list of introductions for the lonely, correspondence courses on graphology and hypnotism, a free "6,000-word treatise" on how to talk with God, and books like *Think and Grow Rich* and *Eugenics and Sex Harmony;* the latter, with "more than 100 vivid pictures," would of course be sent in a plain wrapper.

Two articles in the *Modern Psychologist* must have helped to blur the distinction in the public mind between such inanity and genuine psychology. In one piece a psychologist who had a Ph.D. and belonged to the APA offered readers a self-administered I.Q. test. In the other Henry C. Link of the Psychological Corporation gave an interview on his latest book, *The Return to Religion.* Because the readers of the *Modern Psychologist* believed that psychology belonged to everyone, they probably saw no inherent difference between the articles by real psychologists and the other offerings in the magazine. Moreover, when psychologists tried to write for a popular audience they often became indistinguishable from the less learned contributors to the *Modern Psychologist* and similar publications. Few industrial psychologists, for example, would have found important inaccuracies in "Salesmanship Means Selling Yourself," another piece from the April issue. So applied psychology faced a dilemma. If psychologists wrote for the general public, they might easily become mere popularizers; if they concentrated their efforts on managers and administrators, they could not justifiably complain if others tried to fill the public's needs for psychological counseling.

To solve the puzzle, applied psychologists needed first to win the confidence of educators, physicians, businessmen, and others who might use psychological services. The thirties saw much research on the instruments and techniques of applied psychology. The number and variety of mental tests increased greatly, and devices to measure intelligence, abilities, interests, and personality became standard equipment for the practitioner. The most abstruse of these instruments, the Rorschach test, featured mysterious inkblots, the significance of which could only be known to a trained psychologist. Applied psychology made progress, but it did not produce any startling innovation such as the intelligence test of two decades before. To impress potential employers and enhance their claim to professional status, psychologists needed what they did not discover in the thirties: a technique or device that had wide applicability, worked reliably, and yet remained under their exclusive control. Without it the road to professionalism promised to be long and uncertain.

In the thirties applied psychologists entered a new phase in the battle for higher standards. They fought not only frauds and amateurs but each other as well. The leaders of American psychology maintained a strong commitment to scholarly inquiry and to the doctorate as a sign of competence. The APA took little interest in unemployed holders of master's degrees. Such people were not seen as psychologists nor as likely to become psychologists. The group founded ostensibly for practitioners, the AAAP, pursued even higher academic standards by limiting membership to holders of the Ph.D. The Psychologists League and a minority within the AAAP, on the other hand, doubted that a research degree should be the prerequisite for psychological practice, and they opposed policies that discriminated against those with only an M.A. At the decade's close the controversy continued without the prospect of an early settlement.

The depression produced serious discussion of the job possibilities for psychologists. The vision of a huge unfilled demand for psychological services, especially counseling, led to the hope that unemployment would soon end and that psychiatrists would ultimately fail to exclude psychologists from therapy. Beyond that, however, the dream might become a nightmare for practitioners who wished to maintain professional standards. If, as one estimate suggested, American schools alone needed seventy-five thousand psychological counselors, then all the psychologists in the country—those with M.A.s as well as those with Ph.D.s—could not possibly fill the demand. The future might bring a further dilution of standards and an invasion by people in nearby fields such as education or social work. If this happened, it would come in an effort to meet the great need for the services that psychologists themselves could not fulfill.

If any psychologist had gotten the impression from sociology books that professionalization moved forward by a self-sustaining inner logic, events of the thirties must have disabused him of that notion. Applied psychologists had to work long and hard just to produce a national organization, and they still had no assurance that the AAAP with its exclusiveness and academic orientation would be able to solve their other professional problems. Moreover, psychologists were affected by events beyond their control. Their failure to develop some startling innovation may fall in this category, but the depression provides the obvious example.

The gloomy job market in the thirties brought professional issues to the attention of even the most academically inclined psychologist. As the only employment available for many recent graduates, work in applied fields carried less stigma in 1938 than it had a decade earlier. The APA, the bastion of academic psychology, reversed its position of the twenties, taking up professional issues itself and encouraging the formation of a national organization for practitioners. Despite its shortcomings, the AAAP was the first group that could at least claim to speak and act for the country's applied psychologists. Their efforts to achieve professional status and their responses to the depression meant that in 1938, as never before, psychologists were ready to extend the applications of their discipline. They still needed a broadened demand for their services, however, but that was to come in full measure during the next seven years.

5

PSYCHOLOGISTS AND THE WAR

While the depression dragged on in the United States, war threatened once again in Europe. Like many other Americans, psychologists worried that their country would be drawn unprepared into the conflict. In September 1938 the annual business meeting of the American Association for Applied Psychology responded to the growing European crisis by instructing its leadership to approach the War Department and discuss the role of psychologists in national defense. In a few weeks the war scare passed. The British prime minister, Neville Chamberlain, returned from the Munich conference to declare that his new agreement with Hitler meant "peace for our time." Many Americans, wanting very much to believe Chamberlain's prediction, turned their attention away from military preparedness. The psychologists, however, still saw war looming ahead, and they persisted in their efforts to win a place in the Roosevelt administration's slowly moving rearmament program.

The interest of psychologists in national defense arose from more than mere patriotism. All psychologists knew (and many remembered from their own experience) that the First World War had provided a great impetus to applied psychology. During the war psychologists had developed the group intelligence test and much of personnel psychology, and many people had begun thinking in psychological terms. The past twenty years, however, had not been entirely happy ones for applied psychology; another large-scale mobilization would give psychologists a new chance to display their techniques and perhaps to expand their capabilities. For example, Horace B. English, executive secretary of the AAAP, hoped that psychologists would be given the task of testing and classifying not only military recruits but all Americans. Florence Goodenough of

The bulk of this chapter originally appeared as "The Mobilization of American Psychologists, 1938-1941" in *Military Affairs,* February 1978, 32-36; Copyright 1978 by the American Military Institute and used with permission.

the University of Minnesota saw an opportunity to collect large amounts of unusual data. "The world in time of war," she explained, "provides a kind of psychological laboratory which is never duplicated exactly in peacetime."[1]

Unlike some other scientists, most applied psychologists did not consider military duties a wide diversion from their usual activities. The armed services, like civilian businesses, needed an efficient and reasonably contented work force. Modern warfare demanded not only a great number of men who could march and shoot but also many who could operate complicated equipment and perform esoteric tasks. The problem of putting each man in a productive and congenial job became more difficult than ever before. Although not quite aware of it in 1938, the military needed men who were not just patriotic and highly disciplined but also well adjusted. Facilitating personal adjustment was the applied psychologist's main function in civilian life. Performing that task for the military would be more challenging but not fundamentally different.

While they never used this argument in negotiations with the military, psychologists realized that mobilization would produce many new psychological jobs. The effects of the depression had by no means ended in 1938, and many psychologists needed work. A testing program would not only furnish an important service to the army but would also give unemployed psychologists a chance to perform useful work. Here was an instance in which the needs of psychology would coincide with those of the military.

Not all psychologists expressed unalloyed enthusiasm for work in the national defense. Some objected to cooperating in any venture that might lead the United States into another war. They believed psychologists should work instead to keep the country at peace. Other psychologists feared their discipline would become so involved in applications that pure research would suffer. Introducing a prewar issue of the *Psychological Bulletin* that was devoted entirely to military psychology, Carrol C. Pratt warned his colleagues that "times are changed, and it may be that more psychologists than we realize will be called upon to change their habits of mind and their topics of research."[2]

Such opinions represented only a minority of the discipline. Most psychologists viewed military work as a fortuitous conjunction of duty and opportunity. In the fall of 1941 Gordon Allport, a recent president of the APA, saw fit to remind his colleagues that "working for the introduction of psychologists into national and local services may be helpful to the profession, but it is not necessarily beneficial to the nation." "Pushing psychology forward," he continued, "is not the same thing as pushing the country forward."[3] Allport's distinction probably seemed gratuitous to many psychologists.

The psychologists' campaign to join the army got off to a faltering start. In September 1938 Walter Dill Scott offered to assist the War Department with its classification procedures. Although Scott was one of America's leading industrial psychologists and had virtually invented the army's personnel system in World War 1, he received only a polite refusal. The secretary of war informed him that the army required no help at present and did not foresee needing any in the future. Two months later Horace B. English tried making contact at a lower echelon. He suggested to the adjutant general, Emory S. Adams, that if the mental testing of recruits was to be part of mobilization, now was the time to begin organizing the army's psychological activities. Adams replied that psychology came under the jurisdiction of medical officers, and he referred English to the surgeon general.

American psychologists did not intend to serve again in the Medical Corps. Too many of them—English included—recalled unhappy experiences in the First World War when psychiatrists and other physicians had frustrated efforts to develop psychological testing to its fullest extent. Working under medical officers, English believed, had been a "historical accident" that "resulted in much inefficiency and confusion." If psychology was to have an opportunity to show what it could do, it must operate outside the control of its professional adversaries. English quickly responded to General Adams. Arguing that psychologists belonged in the Adjutant General's Office because most of their past military activities had been in personnel classification, he requested a meeting with a representative of that office at the end of December. Adams raised no further objections and assigned one of his subordinates to talk with English.[4]

Armed with a long memorandum outlining psychology's military uses, English journeyed to Washington to face the army. He told the men from the Adjutant General's Office that psychologists were prepared to help in classifying recruits, selecting men with specific capabilities, analyzing jobs, improving training programs, and bolstering morale. English found that, although his audience had not thought much about using psychologists, they seemed receptive to the idea and asked him to help them find someone to work in Washington with the War Plans Division. English did not sell his entire program, but he did gain a crucial opening for psychology within the military. Because the United States was not to go to war for almost three years, psychologists had plenty of time to expand English's initial contacts. And because the Adjutant General's Office now took charge of psychological testing in the army, psychologists could operate free of any interference by medical officers.

Military psychology made considerable progress in 1939. In the spring the adjutant general took official notice of the need for a new classification test by establishing a personnel testing section. This group appointed an AAAP member as civilian consultant and quickly set to work on a replacement for the old Army Alpha test of World War 1. The goal was a device that would separate recruits into broad categories on the basis of how easily they could be trained. Psychologists knew that they could develop an improved intelligence test, but they also believed that they had far more to contribute to military personnel work. So they spent much of the year in trying to convince the army of their potential. Their efforts to win a wider role achieved some success, and in November, two months after the outbreak of war in Europe, the AAAP had little difficulty in finding military participants for a round-table discussion of the contributions psychology could make in a national emergency. The army sent several representatives, including Major Lewis B. Hershey, who was then working on a plan to implement military conscription.

By April 1940 the Adjutant General's Office decided to seek a panel of civilian consultants to augment its own efforts in psychological testing. In response to its request for aid, there was soon formed the Committee on Classification of Military Personnel. Chaired by Walter Van Dyke Bingham, the committee included some of the most prestigious experts in the fields of testing and personnel. Its other civilian members were Carl C. Brigham of Princeton, Henry C. Garrett of Columbia, Carrol L. Shartle of the Social Security Board, and L. L. Thurstone of the University of Chicago. The committee, faced with growing public agitation for conscription, joined in the work on a classification test. In July Bingham, who would soon assume the title of the army's chief psychologist, gave an optimistic appraisal of the state of military psychology. In a letter to APA members and chairmen of psychology departments, he announced that 1940 would not be like 1917. The army was prepared for psychological examining and convinced of the value of psychologists. If a serious national emergency arose, Bingham continued, psychologists could count on being used in many areas. On 16 September President Roosevelt signed the Selective Service and Training Act. When the first inductees reached army reception centers two months later, the General Classification Test was waiting for them.

The army's testing program was just beginning. The number of psychologists working on military personnel problems continued to grow, expanding rapidly once the United States entered the war. Many varieties of new examinations were developed, including classification tests for women and officer candidates, tests to determine mechanical and clerical aptitude, achievement tests in academic subjects, and tests to measure knowledge of trades. The army administered these examinations by the millions. By the end of the war, for example, some 9 million men—one-seventh of the entire male population of the country—had taken the general classification test. The psychologists' early efforts to make themselves useful to the adjutant general paid a handsome reward, for during the war the army established the largest and most diversified testing program in history.

Probably the single most technically complex task in the military was flying an airplane. Training lasted over a year and was extremely expensive. As long as only a few men entered pilot training each year, the costs of eliminating incompetent students remained low. When the country needed aviators in large numbers, however, the ability to select the most capable men for training became far more critical. A number of agencies outside the Adjutant General's Office worked on the selection of pilots. Their efforts, though not as extensive as the army personnel program, again gave psychologists an opportunity to contribute to national defense. The psychologists began work on pilot selection in 1939 and continued their efforts throughout the war.

During the last week of 1938 President Roosevelt announced an important step in the rearmament program. He proposed that the Civil Aeronautics Authority undertake the training of twenty thousand new pilots on college campuses across the country. If Congress approved, the program was to go into effect in the fall of 1939. Despite its military overtones, the plan achieved immediate popularity. A Gallup poll in January revealed that 87 percent of those interviewed believed the government ought to begin training pilots for national defense. College students showed their enthusiasm for the proposal by volunteering in large numbers. It soon became clear that the number of applicants would exceed the available positions and the government would have to find a way to select the most promising candidates.

It happened that the assistant administrator of the CAA, Dean R. Brimhall, was a psychologist. By the late summer of 1939 Brimhall was planning to set up a program of research on pilot selection and training. On 4 September, one day after England declared war on Germany, he arrived at the APA convention in California to see if he could enlist the aid of his colleagues. He made informal approaches to APA members and found them ready to help but unwilling to involve the association. They suggested that Brimhall contact the National Research Council (NRC) in Washington; its Division of Anthropology and Psychology, they assured him, would be happy to render assistance. Brimhall accepted their advice, and two weeks later the chairman of the CAA formally asked the NRC to establish and administer a research program on pilot selection and training.

It looked as though psychology might be on the verge of helping to reinvigorate the National Research Council. During World War 1 the council had served as a contact point between scientists and the government and had attempted to coordinate research on military problems. In the subsequent twenty years, however, the NRC had lost most of its connection with the government. In the spring of 1939, when the council's psychologists were looking for a chance to join in the defense mobilization, they suspected that no one knew of their existence. They thus welcomed the CAA's initiative and quickly established the Committee on Selection and Training of Civilian Aircraft Pilots within the NRC. The CAA funded the project with a grant of $100,000—a small sum when compared with the government's later wartime expenditures for scientific research but an astronomical amount for psychology in 1939.

The committee at first thought that it would deal mostly with problems of pilot training, but it soon also became involved in questions of performance under stress, measurement of successful learning, and instruments for selection and classification. The CAA never envisioned separate research facilities for these projects. Instead, it instructed the NRC to distribute the work to various university laboratories around the country. This approach allowed the committee great latitude in choosing the most competent researchers and brought for the first time an essentially military problem to the home of academic psychology. *Science News Letter* called the use of university laboratories and personnel "a new departure" in federally sponsored research.[5] In the past the government had almost always provided its own laboratories or scientists. In this instance, however, it maintained little direct control over the projects. When opposition arose in 1940 to extending the committee's work, Brimhall, because of his strategic position within the CAA and his confidence in aviation psychology, was able to assure the continued funding of the program.

As the government's rearmament program intensified, the committee dropped "civilian" from its title and turned most of its attention toward specifically military problems. In the fall of 1941 John G. Jenkins, the committee's research director, outlined some of these activities in an article for the *Journal of Consulting Psychology*. Since the need for military secrecy prevented Jenkins from giving many details, his readers may have been struck more by his optimistic tone than any specific new information. Jenkins was deeply impressed by the cooperation his committee was receiving. Psychologists from thirty universities worked together smoothly. They did research not only in their laboratories but in the sky as well. Over 50 had taken some pilot training and at least 20 received private pilot's licenses. Many became so absorbed in their work that they spent additional hours lingering at airports, immersed in the atmosphere of aviation. Jenkins also took encouragement from a "close, cordial, and effective" liaison with physicians on the NRC and flight surgeons in the military. All conditions favored the committee's success. "If psychologists can indeed aid in selecting, training, and maintaining the pilots required by modern aircraft," he asserted, "they are being offered every facility to demonstrate the fact." The rewards of accomplishment would be great. "As a professional group," he concluded, "we are face to face with an opportunity and an obligation of the first magnitude."[6]

The Committee on Selection and Training of Aircraft Pilots continued its operations throughout the war. By 1945 it had spent more than $900,000, let contracts to over 40 universities and other research centers, and used the facilities of almost 600 additional institutions in carrying out its work. The committee's connection with the NRC did not serve as a precedent for the mobilization of scientists; the government instead established a new group, the National Defense Research Committee (and later the Office of Scientific Research and Development) for this purpose. The committee did, however, act as an initial contact point between many psychologists and the military, giving each group an opportunity to work with and appreciate the other. Organized at the very beginning of the government's rearmament program, the committee allowed psychologists enough time to integrate their scientific interests with the needs of American aviation. The committee's work undoubtedly would have become even more extensive if the armed forces had not decided to establish their own groups for aviation psychology within the military itself.

The air force program in aviation psychology got under way in July 1941. Before that the medical officers who supervised pilot selection had relied on physical examinations, psychiatric interviews, and educational requirements to choose men for flight schools. Civilian psychologists played only a minor, advisory role in this procedure. As rearmament continued and pilot quotas grew, however, it became clear that such personalized methods of pilot selection would become unacceptably cumbersome and expensive. Furthermore, in the decade before the war between 40 and 60 percent of aviation cadets were eliminated from their training programs before graduation. That failure rate, which caused no alarm when the air force needed only a few pilots, foretold a disastrous loss of resources if continued into a war. As it happened, the number of cadets accepted for aviation training would grow from 12 in 1937 to over 293,000 five years later.

In mid-July of 1941 the associate director of the Cooperative Test

Service, John C. Flanagan, accepted a major's commission and became the first psychologist in the air force. He began to organize a psychological research program that was soon to include a central office in Washington and several research units at air bases across the country. One of his first problems was finding experienced men to act as supervisors. The air force could count on the threat of induction and the shriveled civilian job market to produce junior officers and enlisted men, but to lure established psychologists away from their academic posts it needed a further inducement—the direct commission. Like the other services, the air force used this means to recruit many of its senior men. By the fall Flanagan had found psychologists to lead his subordinate units, the first of which opened in September.

The next few months saw important changes in the aviation psychology program. Some highly placed air force officers advocated replacing the educational requirements for pilot selection with an intelligence and aptitude test. While anxious to be useful, aviation psychologists realized that they had as yet no reliable method to measure pilot aptitude. They proposed that they develop a general test to choose all aviation cadets—navigators and bombardiers as well as pilots—and that the air force postpone selecting men for specific air crew positions until they had completed the first part of their training. "In making these proposals," Flanagan later explained, "the psychological research group had clearly decided to abandon its purely research role and to recommend practical procedures for immediate use even though these procedures would necessarily be initially without adequate research foundation."[7]

The air force adopted these recommendations in December and set up several hundred aviation cadet examining boards throughout the country. The first version of the general selection test also appeared in December. A month later a board of generals appointed by the commander of the air force approved a revised form, and the Aviation Cadet Qualifying Examination went into effect. A multiple-choice test with items drawn as much as possible from situations that cadets might encounter in training, it was designed, explained one of the air force's leading testers, "to select men sufficiently literate to become officers and sufficiently endowed with certain aptitudes to graduate from flying training, especially pilot training."[8] By the end of the war well over 1 million men had taken one of the many revisions of the test.

Meanwhile aviation psychologists were trying to develop a series of examinations that would help to weed out the potential navigators and bombardiers from the potential pilots. During the war the psychologists constructed, administered, and often discarded a large number of such devices. They continued to worry about the basic flaw in their testing program: potential ability in combat ought to have been the primary criterion for selecting flyers, but because of the great time lapse between taking the tests and entering combat as well as the difficulty in determining what constituted competence in battle, the examinations could predict only who was likely to complete training successfully. In 1943 the aviation psychology program expanded its research to include evaluation of air crew proficiency and related problems. When the war ended, however, the psychologists had yet to plug this hole in their testing program.

Psychologists in the air force continued to expand their activities throughout the war. In the four years after Flanagan received his commission, the aviation psychology program grew to include 200 officers, 750 enlisted persons, and 500 civilians. Perhaps a third of those serving in uniform held advanced degrees. Like their colleagues in other aspects of the war effort, air force psychologists accepted a wide variety of tasks, many of which went beyond their civilian experience. By the end of the war they found themselves counseling men in convalescent hospitals, helping to choose gunnery instructors, analyzing the job attitudes of enlisted men, and performing other duties far removed from their academic preparation. Although sometimes disappointed with their accomplishments, air force psychologists never lost confidence in the ability of their science to aid in human adjustment.

Applied psychology in the navy developed along lines that were different from those in the army and air force. When the AAAP convened its round-table discussion of psychology and the national emergency in November 1939, the navy sent Captain Dallas G. Sutton of the Medical Corps. Sutton had no doubts about the potential value of psychologists in the navy, but he did not envision a large-scale, centrally planned testing program. Instead, he believed psychologists would be used to help medical officers in the individual examination of recruits.[9] Although this was exactly the procedure that psychologists found so offensive in the army, they raised no sustained objections. Perhaps they had no unpleasant memories of naval duty in World War 1, lacked suitable contacts with navy personnel men, or thought the navy, which enlisted only volunteers, had less need for testing. In any case, after close consultation between Sutton and the chairman of the AAAP's Committee on Relations with the Medical Profession, the navy's program began to take form in the fall of 1940.

The navy acquired its first psychologist, C. M. Louttit of Indiana University, in October 1940. If it were looking for a man with wide contacts among applied psychologists, the navy could hardly have done better than Louttit, who was then the executive secretary of the AAAP. Operating from the Naval Medical School in Washington, Louttit began planning for the use of psychologists at training stations. One of his first tasks was recruiting experienced men. Because of his position in the AAAP Louttit was able to peruse the association's files to find the names of likely candidates. He then wrote and invited them to apply for commissions. Louttit's superiors in the navy appreciated his use of AAAP files. Only a few association members expressed any concern about involving the AAAP in military recruitment, and Louttit continued to believe both the navy and the association benefited from his activity.

Late in 1940 the navy established a new branch of the Medical Corps for psychologists and other nonmedical specialists. Soon thereafter the first psychologists received their assignments to neuropsychiatric boards at basic training stations. There they were to examine each recruit whose initial test scores gave an indication that he might be unfit for service. They were to test not only for abilities but also for traits of feeling and temperament. The navy gave its psychologists wide latitude in carrying out these two duties, especially the latter. "Methods of evaluating temperamental traits by means of psychological methods are not specified," Louttit reported, "largely because of the lack of entirely satisfactory instruments."[10] By the spring of 1941 the use of psychologists on neuropsychiatric boards was well under way.

Meanwhile the navy was launching a program of aviation psychology. The NRC's Committee on Selection and Training of Aircraft Pilots had been working on problems of naval aviation for about a year when the committee's research director, John G. Jenkins, went on active duty and took command of the new program. In July 1941 he set to work to fill the recently authorized quotas for aviation psychologists. The psychologists were to become involved in cadet training at every step, from serving on the recruit's initial selection board to helping to make the new pilot's specific assignment. Administering tests was the psychologists' main duty, but they conducted interviews and performed some research as well. Compared with aviation psychology in the air force, the navy's program relied less on centralized planning and put less emphasis on the development of new tests.

Psychologists in the navy often found themselves left to their own initiative. Operating at a variety of naval installations, they received limited guidance from their superiors in Washington and little initial understanding from their local commanders. Aviation psychologists, Jenkins reported, "arrived at peripheral training activities (pre-fight schools, flight preparatory schools, primary training bases, gunnery schools, etc.) unable to define their own place in the military organization and unable to find anyone else who could define it." Testing consumed only a few hours a week, and psychologists soon began accepting new duties—some far removed from their academic preparation—for which their background and training might in some way prepare them. "Almost to a man," Jenkins observed, "they discarded any worry as to whether a given task was appropriate for a Ph.D. or for a psychologist and began to weave themselves firmly into the local fabric."[11] Psychologists on cadet selection boards had similar experiences. In both assignments they had to carve out a place for themselves in naval aviation.

The psychologists who worked on neuropsychiatric boards faced a slightly different situation from that of their colleagues in naval aviation. Beyond a general mandate to test, their duties depended largely on the psychiatrists for whom they worked. If they could show their usefulness—as a great many did—their responsibilities expanded. The use of clinical psychologists at naval hospitals, for example, began on an informal basis because specific doctors had confidence in individual psychologists. Even when the navy began formally assigning clinical psychologists to hospitals, their range of duties remained dependent on their competence and initiative. William A. Hunt, one of the navy's highest ranking psychologists, believed that the lack of centralized control brought undeniable benefits. "Clinical psychology in the Navy," he explained, "has been marked by a rugged individualism which has been invaluable in meeting the constantly changing exigencies of the war."[12]

Despite the opportunity for heightened professional animosities, most of the navy's psychologists got along well enough in the Medical Corps. World War 1 did not repeat itself. First, the value of psychological testing was much more apparent to physicians and local commanders in 1941 than it had been in 1917. In addition, the Medical Corps itself needed little convincing: it planned as early as 1939 to recruit psychologists, and it established a generous commissioning policy (about 95 percent of its psychologists served as officers) that left few embittered enlisted men. Finally, the psychologists had improved their techniques between the wars, and when they went on active duty they were ready and willing to show what they could do. Whatever the explanation, the "rugged individualism" of 1941 produced an expanded use of both aviation and clinical psychologists as the war continued.

By the time the United States entered the war, the navy had several dozen psychologists operating at bases across the country. It did not, however, have a centralized test development program like the one in the Adjutant General's Office of the army. The tests used before Pearl Harbor soon proved inadequate to classify the flood of new recruits. Some testers at local units tried to develop their own examinations, but the task clearly fell beyond their resources. In the spring of 1942 the problem reached the

Bureau of Naval Personnel, which responded by initiating its own work on test research and by requesting aid from the Office of Scientific Research and Development (OSRD). The navy's need for psychological help provided psychologists with an entering wedge into the wartime scientific establishment. Although civilian psychologists had been engaged in military research since 1939, with the exception of their use by the CAA the government had not attempted to mobilize them on a large scale. Individual psychologists worked on projects for the OSRD but remained under the supervision of other researchers. The dispersion of psychological activities came to the attention of Leonard Carmichael, a recent APA president and currently director of an agency that was collecting data on all American scientists. In March 1942 Carmichael wrote to Vannevar Bush, head of the OSRD, and suggested that Bush's office set up a central liaison group for psychological research.

Officials of the OSRD informed Carmichael that the office had no objection in principle to military psychology but that it was unwilling to establish an agency for psychology or any other discipline without the assurance of support by high-ranking military officers. Carmichael and his associates now had the task of generating a demand for psychological services which existing groups did not already fill. This might have been an insurmountable obstacle in the fall of 1938, but by the spring of 1942 it provided no serious problem. Ties between psychologists and the military were now close and varied. Carmichael quickly produced two naval officers who were concerned with the development of new aptitude tests and were in positions to see that psychological research would be put to use.

In June, following a formal request by the navy, the OSRD established what became the Applied Psychology Panel. Although the new agency never provided the centralized coordination that Carmichael envisioned, it did give many civilian psychologists a chance to share in the war effort. Like the committee working for the CAA, the panel let contracts for specific projects; unlike the committee, it did most of its work at military bases rather than college campuses. The panel initiated projects only in response to specific requests from the military, and it tried to avoid competing with work already under way within the armed forces. The projects, which might employ as many as a dozen psychologists, usually produced results within a year.

In its first year the panel concentrated on problems of classification. Then as the war continued, the emphasis shifted toward work on the selection and training of such specialists as radar operators, night lookouts, and naval gunners. Research even extended to the inanimate half of what was sometimes called the "man-machine unit." A few psychologists attempted to redesign equipment—a field artillery gunsight, for example—in order to bring it more into accordance with psychological principles. During the war the panel set up twenty major projects, employed some two hundred psychologists, published over five hundred reports, and spent more than $1.5 million. It might even have expanded its activities if it had been able to find more academicians who could take the time to supervise its projects.

The panel's greatest impact came in its work on personnel testing for the navy. The project got under way in September 1942 and featured very close cooperation with the navy's own psychologists. In March 1943 five new tests—general classification, reading, arithmetic reasoning, mechanical knowledge, and mechanical aptitude—were ready for experimental use. In June the Basic Test Battery went into routine administration at all naval training stations. During the next two years some 2 million recruits began their navy careers by taking this series of tests. Meanwhile psychological work within the Bureau of Naval Personnel expanded greatly. An evergrowing staff, with the aid of psychologists provided by the Applied Psychology Panel, produced over 250 different tests by the end of the war.

Generally, psychological work on military problems followed a single pattern of development: initial contact early in the rearmament program, fairly quick acceptance of psychology by military leaders, and continual growth until the end of the war. Personnel work in the navy provided something of an exception because operations did not get under way until the autumn of 1942. But it was in the army's use of clinical psychologists that the longest delays occurred. Professional rivalries and opposition within the military seriously hampered the program, which did not begin to fill the army's needs until 1945. As in the case of other branches of military psychology, much of the explanation for wartime developments lay in the prewar period of mobilization. As in the past, the utilization of clinical psychologists largely depended on the social role of psychiatry and the needs of individual psychiatrists.

From the opening maneuvers to join the Adjutant General's Office, psychologists sought independence from psychiatry. In May 1939 Horace B. English, then executive secretary of the AAAP, suggested that the organization oppose any use of clinical psychologists within the army's Medical Division which did not grant them equality in diagnosis with physicians. English conceded that such an unacceptable condition would mean the reduced utilization of psychology—and presumably a decline in patients' welfare—but he believed this would be more than offset by the "healthier status for the growth of clinical psychology" which would result. Nor was English mollified by the thought that clinical psychologists might individually develop productive and harmonious relations with the psychiatrists for whom they worked. He believed it was "humiliating and undignified for psychology to be dependent on such personal victory."[13]

The AAAP did not act on English's proposal until September 1940, when he restated his views before a meeting of the Clinical Section. After a lengthy discussion the section resolved that clinical psychologists should not be assigned to the Medical Department but should serve primarily in organizations working in the fields of personnel and morale. This position was controversial, for some psychologists opposed divorcing clinical psychology from medicine. They believed that the unhappy experiences of World War 1 would not repeat themselves and that the psychologists in the Adjutant General's Office should have tried to set up a program for clinical work similar to the one in the navy.

The psychologists' role in the Adjutant General's Department expanded in 1941. At the beginning of the year the army established a program to train and use psychologists as "personnel consultants." The quota for 1941 was set at one hundred. Initially these psychologists served at induction centers and basic training camps, but with the continued growth of the army, personnel consultants were assigned to special training centers for slow learners, jails, and other units. In addition, each division and higher echelon of command had a personnel consultant to assist the adjutant. As the war continued, duties expanded from merely giving tests into a variety of new fields. Personnel consultants interviewed soldiers, provided counseling on personal problems, conducted group psychotherapy, prepared classes for illiterates, and gave lectures on military psychology. To an increasing extent personnel consultants became involved in varieties of clinical work.

In the spring of 1942, however, no clinical psychologists were serving in hospitals under the supervision of psychiatrists. In part this was due to the psychologists' opposition to such service, in part to the limited role the army assigned to psychiatry. During the period of mobilization, when psychologists were developing tests for the adjutant general, psychiatrists were assuring the Medical Department that they could screen out most mentally unstable recruits at the induction centers. Thus the army made no plans to use psychiatrists in hospitals, and it understandably saw no need for clinical psychologists there either. In June 1941 a committee of the National Research Council recommended that the Medical Department provide openings for psychologists, but the surgeon general ignored the recommendation.

As the size of the army grew and more men entered combat, the number of neuropsychiatric casualties increased. It soon became obvious that the psychiatric interview at induction, which seldom lasted over three minutes, could weed out only the severely disturbed recruits. Psychiatrists now realized that they could not predict which otherwise normal men would crack under the strain of military duties. Psychiatric wards filled and the demand for clinical psychologists grew. In the spring of 1942 the surgeon general commissioned six psychologists in the Sanitary Corps as an "experiment" and assigned them to army hospitals. Although these men soon found useful work to do, they were not joined by any colleagues. The army's psychiatrists did not have sufficient influence to expand the program in the face of the hostility or indifference that other physicians showed to psychiatric problems and the strong objections that psychologists had to assignment in the Medical Department. Some personnel consultants drifted into hospital work, and enlisted men with psychological training were also pressed into service. But the army developed no unified program for the use of clinical psychologists until 1944.

For over half the war the army considered psychiatric problems less as war wounds than as personality defects. The surgeon general saw little need to provide treatment for men who could not withstand the stresses of military life, and the psychiatrist's main task became diagnosing cases and finding suitable categories under which men could receive discharges. Often these former soldiers then entered civilian mental institutions that were neither willing nor able to help them. As the war continued and America's reserves of civilian manpower dwindled, the army began to consider salvaging some of the many maladjusted soldiers who were receiving discharges. In November 1943 the army reversed the policy of routinely granting discharges to soldiers with psychiatric disorders. Gradually civilian complaints and military needs combined to produce a larger emphasis on treatment and thus a greater demand for clinical psychologists. In 1944 President Roosevelt formalized the new policy when he instructed the secretary of war "to insure that no overseas casualty is discharged from the armed forces until he has received the maximum benefits of hospitalization and convalescent facilities which must include . . . psychological rehabilitation, . . ."[14]

Meanwhile clinical psychology obtained a powerful new advocate in the Surgeon General's Office when in December 1943 Colonel William C. Menninger became the chief of the neuropsychiatric branch. Menninger, who before the war had consistently employed psychologists at his clinic in Topeka, Kansas, moved quickly to expand psychiatric services in the army. In one of his first actions he opened negotiations with the adjutant general to find a method of assigning more psychologists to clinical work.

In mid-1944 a three-point plan emerged. First, the Medical Department agreed that all clinical psychologists should be assigned to the Adjutant General's Office, where they would serve under the administrative control of the newly created office of the chief clinical psychologist. Second, the adjutant general reassigned 130 psychologists from other duties to clinical work. Finally, the army bolstered the program by commissioning some 250 enlisted men who had had training and experience in clinical psychology.

The duties of a clinical psychologist in the army sounded much like those of his civilian colleague. The job description stated that the clinical psychologist interviewed patients, administered and interpreted tests, diagnosed illnesses and made recommendations for further action, and assisted in guidance and psychotherapy. As in civilian life, the exact nature of each psychologist's work—especially his work in therapy—depended in large measure on the trust afforded him by his supervising psychiatrist. The growing number of neuropsychiatric patients, however, altered this relationship to some extent. Finding themselves overworked, psychiatrists increasingly passed some of their cases (aphasics, for example) on to the clinical psychologists for treatment.

Clinical psychologists discovered other differences between civilian and military practice. The army did not have the resources to permit deep probing into the psychological problems presented by all of its 1 million neuropsychiatric patients. What distinguished clinical psychology in the military, explained Morton A. Seidenfeld, the army's chief clinical psychologist, was "the use of simple and brief procedures as contrasted with techniques requiring an extensive outlay of time."[15] Psychology's traditional orientation toward the amelioration of immediate problems proved easily adaptable to military needs. The psychologist's place on the clinical team, which had been threatened by the growing popularity of Freudianism in the thirties, became secure once again. The army also presented a different sort of patient: the young adult, often suffering from mild disturbances, who had grown up in places untouched by clinical psychology. Work in psychotherapy increased, and in 1945 clinical psychologists were spending an average of 25 percent of their time treating patients.

The ultimate goal of clinical work in the army varied somewhat from that in civilian life. Because the needs of the military always took precedence over those of the patients, the clinician was required to send as many men as possible back to active duty. In many cases, of course, the return might not be in the soldier's best interests. Psychologists never became overly concerned with this problem of divided loyalties, however. They not only held a firm commitment to the war effort, but they also understood the social imperatives entailed in the notion of adjustment.

In their efforts to restore each cog in the military machine, clinical psychologists were performing a type of personnel work. Their assignment to the Adjutant General's Office as personnel consultants was thus not as anomalous as it might first appear.

Only in the summer of 1945 did the supply of clinical psychologists catch up with the demand. By then 450 clinical psychologists were serving in the army. Two-thirds of this number worked in general, station, and convalescent hospitals, and others were assigned to correctional institutions and basic training centers. The army's program for clinical psychologists, which in size and variety had no civilian counterpart, featured an unusual amount of cooperation and good feeling between psychologists and psychiatrists. Some professional rivalry arose, but many psychologists found that their subordinate position did not interfere with the performance of useful and rewarding work. Referring to its "symbiotic support of neuropsychiatry," Seidenfeld declared that psychology had "written an illustrious chapter in the Medical Department."[16]

The war provided psychologists an unprecedented opportunity to work in new capacities and unusual settings. A large number of agencies established programs that used psychologists. Some of this activity fell within the usual bounds of applied psychology—testing in the merchant marine, for example, or clinical work in the Veterans Administration.

Many psychologists, however, held jobs that were not specifically psychological in nature. This was true for some kinds of personnel work. The War Manpower Commission, for instance, used psychologists in analyzing the nature and requirements of civilian and military jobs. The program, previously a function of the United States Employment Service, had been the government's chief employer of psychologists during the thirties. But its director, himself a psychologist and a member of the APA and the AAAP, conceded that the duties of the psychologists could not be distinguished from those of the other specialists he supervised.

Survey research was another important field in which psychologists worked but did not establish an exclusive domain. The Department of Agriculture began examining popular attitudes in 1936, and three years later it brought in a noted social psychologist, Rensis Likert, to head an expanded program. Likert saw profound implications for public opinion sampling and hoped it would provide "a new technique for making administration more democratic."[17] During the war other agencies accepted this notion and established groups to conduct survey research. Several important policies—on selling war bonds, reinstituting rationing, and funding the G. I. bill, for example—were based in part on information obtained through opinion sampling. All this activity did not necessarily mean more jobs for psychologists, however. Sociologists, economists, and anthropologists also claimed a share of survey research, and by the end of the war social psychologists found that the borders of their discipline had blurred considerably.

On the whole, civilian agencies had fewer jobs specifically for psychologists than did the military, whose need continued to grow. In late 1942 the army concluded that it would soon run out of men with psychological training. It did not, however, anticipate any decline in the growth of psychological work. To meet the expected shortage the army in the spring of 1943 established an intensive undergraduate-level training program for enlisted men in personnel psychology. The courses were given not at military installations but on eleven college campuses throughout the country. Regular faculty members in America's most prestigious departments taught the classes from a standard syllabus. The program served to break down further the crumbling wall between academe and practical military problems. About 150 teachers received an opportunity to contribute to the war effort, and more important perhaps, the government subsidized college training in psychology for the first time. By early 1944 some 1,300 men had completed the twenty-four-week course.

The establishment of the special training program did not indicate a lack of success in recruiting civilian psychologists. During the war about one-fourth of America's psychologists served in uniform. Holders of doctorates joined the military in the same proportion as those with less education. Almost two-thirds of all male psychologists under the age of thirty-eight entered military service, a substantially higher percentage than among the general population. The high rate of participation indicated that psychologists were ready to follow through on their initial enthusiasm for military preparedness. They continued to see work for the armed forces as an opportunity as well as a responsibility.

Psychologists did encounter some problems in their military service. Since superior officers were often unaware of what psychology could do, psychologists were forced to win approval for their techniques before they could achieve some latitude in their work. They needed to gear their presentations to their audiences by giving simple explanations that used graphs and pictures. As one psychologist recalled, "a very little psychology often went a very long way."[18] Operating in a large authoritarian bureaucracy annoyed some psychologists. They doubted that their superiors possessed enough knowledge about psychology to make informed decisions on psychological activity. While most psychologists felt satisfied with their military experience, only 2 percent of them in 1945 planned to stay in uniform after the war ended.

Military psychology's most serious shortcoming may well have been its lack of centralized control. "Eagerness and willingness were abundant," declared Walter Van Dyke Bingham; "but not a little professional talent went to waste for lack of a sufficiently broad national overview of total needs and resources."[19] Psychologists in various agencies duplicated one another's efforts while leaving important problems unsolved. The CAA, the navy, and the air force all developed tests for choosing pilots, for example, but none ever succeeded in validating the tests against performance. The National Defense Research Committee, which coordinated scientific work in other fields, provided little central guidance for psychology. In this case, the psychologists' early start may have hurt them. By the time the committee was established, much of the psychological work on military problems had already been allotted among other agencies.

Psychologists failed to achieve any dramatic breakthrough in technique that might have served to enhance their professional status. "The war," noted one observer, "did not produce revolutionary changes either in the conception of tests or in the nature of psychotherapeutic treatment."[20] For example, the search for a personality test that could predict leadership ability or reactions to combat proved fruitless. Psychologists did, however, gain an unprecedented opportunity to discover the possibilities and limitations of their techniques. Because of their wide experience in the military, testers and clinicians knew more about their work in 1945 than they did before the war.

Some psychologists might argue that shortcomings in technique occurred because of deficiencies in theory. The war, however, produced no theoretical discoveries and very little basic research. Military psychology, commented Charles W. Bray of the Applied Psychology Panel, "contributed little to an increased understanding of the human being but much to the efficiency of use of the human being."[21] When working for the military, psychologists saw their job as applying the technology of human engineering. They concluded that plain psychology, unfettered by theoretical preconceptions, brought results. The experience of the navy's aviation psychologists suggested to John G. Jenkins that "the common core of psychological knowledge and technique is more effective in meeting practical problems of human behavior than are the preachments of any particular point of view."[22] For the duration of the war psychology lost its academic orientation and became an applied science.

From the viewpoint of applied psychology, the Second World War presented the most serious adjustment problem in American history. But it also provided applied psychologists with a crucial opportunity to display the effectiveness of their techniques. They knew that if they could make a significant contribution to the war effort, they would raise their standing in the eyes of potential employers, professional adversaries, academic psychologists, and the public in general. By the end of the war applied psychologists had good reason to believe that they had proved themselves and had thus won many doubters to their cause.

The continued growth of military psychology provides evidence that psychologists were gaining much appreciation for their work. After the initial wave of skepticism their superiors requested psychologists in increasing numbers. Commenting in *Harper's* on the expansion of the psychologists' activities in the Adjutant General's Office, Bingham pointed out that "no one is thrusting all this psychological service upon the Army unasked."[23] Demand for psychologists exceeded supply throughout the war. Moreover, the psychologists themselves thought that the military generally assigned them appropriate work to do. Surveys revealed that on the whole they were much less dissatisfied with their utilization than the physicists, chemists, and geologists who served in the armed forces. Thus both the psychologists and their superiors viewed military psychology as an important tool.

The utilization of psychologists within the military increased largely because the armed services truly needed assistance in ameliorating the problems of adjustment. During World War 2 the army and the navy organized the two largest bureaucracies in American history. Between them they enlisted one-eighth of the entire population of the country. With a group of such size and diversity, the task of efficient organization reached unprecedented proportions. Compounding the problem, modern warfare demanded well-trained workers who could perform highly specialized tasks. The success of the war effort depended to no small degree on how well each person could be fitted into the right job and kept working at it until victory was achieved. In this field as in others military leaders needed expert help to rationalize their procedures. Once they became convinced that psychologists could in some measure apply the principles of science to difficult personnel problems, the place of military psychology was assured.

The strongest claims for psychology's role in the scientific mobilization came from Lybrand Palmer Smith, an engineer and for most of the war the navy's representative on the National Defense Research Committee. "The work of our psychologists," he declared, "permeated every field," making "the 'man-machine' a fighting unit more effective in the air, on the land, on the sea, and under the sea." Smith considered psychologists among the most important experts at the military's disposal. "I believe," he continued, "that the application of psychology in selecting and training men, and in guiding the design of weapons so they would fit men, did more to help win this war than any other single intellectual activity."[24] Psychologists never said such things about themselves, but they were undoubtedly pleased to hear others say them.

Applied psychologists ended the war in much higher repute than they had begun it. The army's chief psychiatrist, William C. Menninger, praised the psychologists' contribution to neuropsychiatry and saw a continuing role for psychologists in clinical work. More surprising, perhaps, were the commendations of military officers. In 1945, for example, the commanding general of the air force gave his strong approval to the aviation psychology program. It had, he stated, "paid off in time, lives, and money saved" and "aided in the establishment of an effective combat air force." And, he added, it had cost relatively little.[25] Such appraisals could not have been lost on either the psychologists themselves or on their potential peacetime employers.

Far more than the depression World War 2 strengthened the psychologists' interest in the applications of their science. The war effort, by providing hundreds of new jobs in applied fields, effectively ended the unemployment of the thirties and created a strong new peacetime demand. Meanwhile a new group of psychologists, less committed to academic careers and interprofessional rivalry, rose to prominence. In 1940, for example, Morton A. Seidenfeld did not possess the scholarly credentials for full APA membership; as a clinician he could not even be considered for the prestigious Society of Experimental Psychologists. Yet five years later Seidenfeld, as the army's chief clinical psychologist, was administering the largest program of psychologists in American history.

The war erased some of the distinctions between academic and applied psychology. Many academicians put aside their own experiments for the duration of the war and worked instead on practical military problems. Involvement in applied psychology became for them a patriotic duty and an opportunity to join in the national war effort. Military projects, moreover, often turned out to be more stimulating than the academicians had anticipated. Many psychologists came to believe that artificial distinctions between science and technology ought not to be perpetuated in psychological organizations. Thus some of the feelings of unity engendered by the war were to show themselves in the psychologists' wartime organizational activities.

All in all, the applied psychologists' experiences during the war more than fulfilled their expectations. Their early involvement and genuine enthusiasm brought them new prestige among their colleagues and increased recognition from the public in general and prospective employers in particular. After almost seven years of work applied psychologists felt a strong sense of accomplishment and self-confidence. The future, although not quite in focus, looked bright. If they could become effectively organized, applied psychologists, by helping Americans adjust to the postwar world, might yet gain the professional status for which they had strived so long.

6

PREPARATIONS FOR PROSPERITY

"The future of psychology," C. M. Louttit told his colleagues in 1943, "can no more be like its past than the Iowa farm boy can be uninfluenced by months spent in Tunisia or Guadalcanal."[1] The war brought many changes to American psychologists. It provided them new jobs, enhanced their feelings of importance, and increased public awareness of their services. While the imperatives of modern warfare were dictating the expanded use of psychology in the construction and maintenance of a military machine, the psychologists themselves were in a position to seize many new opportunities to prove their worth. Because of the early contacts between military officers and leading applied psychologists, military psychology remained firmly in the hands of genuine psychologists who were committed to high professional standards.

Like many other psychologists, Louttit worried that professional prosperity would not continue once peace returned. Only concerted planning, he believed, could insure that psychology would not fall back into the depressed conditions of the thirties. Although specific professional issues remained important, the future of psychology seemed to rest ultimately on maintaining the unity that the war had brought to psychologists. "Until we have co-operation, mutual understanding, and helpfulness among ourselves," Louttit concluded, "we cannot hope to convince the public or our nonpsychological professional colleagues that we are sufficiently mature as a profession to undertake any contribution toward alleviating the many problems of mankind."[2] The achievement of professional status, in short, depended on permanently lowering the barriers between academicians and practitioners.

In the prewar period the national organization devoted primarily to professional issues was the American Association for Applied Psychology. Formed in 1937 as a beneficiary of the American Psychological Association's commonwealth-of-nations policy of the mid-thirties, the AAAP was slowly beginning to move on a variety of fronts. Membership grew nicely in the first few years, the different sections had committees working on professional problems, and state affiliates were organizing practitioners who could not meet the association's high membership standards. The success of the AAAP's executive secretary in getting psychologists assigned to the Adjutant General's Office might have justified the existence of the AAAP even if it had accomplished nothing else. In the period before wartime utilization overshadowed all other issues, many practitioners looked to the AAAP to solve the persistent problems of uniform training, certification, public relations, and ethical conduct.

Practitioners generally agreed that colleges provided inadequate training in applied psychology at both the undergraduate and graduate levels. In 1939 John G. Jenkins, then at the University of Maryland, argued that undergraduate curricula gave only haphazard consideration to applied fields. Applied psychology had, he declared, "continually been forced to beg for crumbs at the table of its genteel—but often shabby—relative, 'pure psychology.'" But the expansion of technological literature in psychology and the formation of the AAAP had encouraged Jenkins to reorient the program in his department toward explaining the theoretical underpinnings of applied work. The emphasis on psychotechnology, he hoped, would furnish a firm, research-oriented basis for later practical work. The program at Maryland and a similar development at Purdue suggested to Jenkins that "the tide has turned and that instruction in psychotechnology will take its place as a natural center for programs of instruction at appropriate universities."[3] It was an optimistic forecast at best.

Graduate programs in psychology were only slightly better adapted to applied fields than those at the undergraduate level. Clinical psychologists, whose work underwent persistent scrutiny from psychiatrists and social workers, showed special interest in redesigning graduate training. Current programs, Carl Rogers of the Rochester Child Guidance Center explained in 1939, "aimed to produce the academic and research individual rather than the psychologist whose primary interest is in the field of dealing with people." One start to solving the problem lay in awarding the practitioner a doctor of psychology degree rather than a Ph.D. Rogers favored this approach, but he also emphasized the personal characteristics that a graduate program must instill in students. Courses should help the student in understanding his own problems and developing "a definite and satisfying philosophy of living." Beyond course work, Rogers believed that graduate programs needed to include a well-planned internship that would furnish a year of supervised experience.[4] Most members of the AAAP probably favored a program similar to the one Rogers suggested. The problem rested with their colleagues of a more scientific orientation who controlled most of the country's psychology departments. Despite the new interest in nonacademic work produced by the depression, few departments in 1939 were ready to redesign traditional programs or soften their academic rigor. Applied psychologists never lost hope; some progress had been made, and the benefits to professionalization promised to be great. "When the time comes that we have developed a training program such as has been described, . . ." Rogers predicted, "there will be no need to fight for improved professional status or to bemoan the inequalities that exist between clinical psychology and other service professions such as psychiatry."[5]

Practitioners also believed that something ought to be done about certification, but they could not agree on what specific moves to make. The main issues remained much as they had in the twenties. Applied psychologists could make a successful claim to professional status only when they had distinguished themselves from the frauds and the incompetents. As long as college training in psychology remained diverse, academic degrees could not indicate levels of skill; other criteria, however, provided an even less certain means of differentiation. Although most members of the AAAP probably preferred the Ph.D. as the chief sign of a qualified psychologist, such a standard was clearly unrealistic at a time when most practitioners did not hold doctorates and most employers could not afford a psychologist with so much training.

Applied psychologists also had to decide who ought to do the certifying. Should it be the states or a professional organization? The APA Clinical Section had tried the second alternative during the twenties, and applied psychology had spent the next decade recovering from the attempt. Nevertheless, self-certification still had its advocates. This approach kept the setting of standards entirely in the hands of psychologists themselves; it allowed flexibility so that requirements could change as applied psychology changed; and it bypassed objections by medical groups that opposed public recognition of psychological practice. The perennial question of self-certification remained: how was a professional organization to enforce its standards on nonmembers without the coercive power of the state?

The other alternative offered troubles as well. In 1941 only about half the states provided any recognition to applied psychologists. In many of these instances the laws referred only to the use of psychologists in committing people to mental institutions. In addition, the school boards of several states had established standards for school psychologists. But no state restricted a term like "consulting psychologist" to practitioners who had passed a state examination, and none ever considered issuing a license to everyone engaged in psychological practice. Prospects for the future of governmental certification looked dim. Gaining legal recognition for applied psychologists required action by psychological organizations in specific states. Only about a quarter of the states had such organizations, and they had to rely on their own initiative and resources. In 1939 the AAAP provided some help by publishing a model certification act for state affiliates that might be contemplating a legislative campaign. Few groups accepted the challenge however, and a survey in 1941 revealed only two states in which there was immediate hope for legal certification.

One of these states was Illinois, where a certification bill had recently cleared the senate before dying in the lower house. A member of the Illinois Society of Consulting Psychologists warned fellow AAAP members about the problems they would encounter in legislative lobbying. For example, they must forestall the potential opposition of other service groups by defining psychology in terms of its methods rather than its duties. To be successful, applied psychologists would need a vigorous, knowledgeable sponsor in the legislature and could expect to spend much time educating lawmakers and the public about professional psychology. They also needed to be able to counter the arguments made against certification, among them that psychologists were too few for such elaborate procedures, that the public would be misled to believe psychologists could diagnose physiological disorders, and that certification did not prevent charlatans from continuing their practice. Psychologists should also expect concerted opposition from physicians. In Illinois the state chapter of the American Medical Association lobbied against the certification measure after putting it on a list of "quack legislative bills."[6]

Neither approach to certification showed much promise in the years before Pearl Harbor. Both suffered from public indifference to the psychologists' quest for professional status. Applied psychologists could not establish an effective certification program until they achieved support from outside their ranks. Only when clients, employers, and practitioners in allied fields saw a need for guaranteeing the competence of psychologists was certification likely to succeed.

Some AAAP members advocated immediate steps to improve applied psychology's public image. One idea was a psychological magazine, on the order of the American Medical Association's *Hygeia*, that would be designed for the layman. Another member suggested that the AAAP hire a public relations man. In 1941 the organization finally published a membership directory that provided the public with the names and addresses of qualified applied psychologists Beyond that only a little was done. The AAAP formed a public relations committee in 1939, abolished it in 1940, and reestablished it in 1941. Despite the importance of its task, the committee never reported any accomplishments or even any activity.

The formulation of an ethical code was another item on the applied psychologists' list of professional priorities. In 1940 a committee of the AAAP's Industrial and Business Section proposed such a code. It dealt with the conflicting obligations to employer and public, and it enjoined psychologists not to lose sight of their ultimate professional virtue—service to humanity—in the quest of other rewards. The code prohibited the misuse of psychological instruments or findings in commercial undertakings and generally required psychologists to retain their scientific objectivity in all situations. The main flaw in the code came in its final article: violations might be penalized merely by expulsion from the section. As always, a code could be no more potent than the organization that promulgated it. Ejection from the AAAP or one of its sections would not provide sufficiently drastic punishment to deter unscrupulous practitioners.

The AAAP suffered from organizational shortcomings that hampered its effectiveness in dealing with professional issues. Membership, although growing, remained too small to finance large-scale operations. The 1941 budget, for example, projected only $3,750 in total income. The division of the association into four overlapping sections led to a duplication and diffusion of effort. "It has never been clear," observed the first executive secretary, Horace B. English, "how the Sections and the Association as a whole are to be integrated." His successor, C. M. Louttit, believed that excessive compartmentalization might require a general reorganization of the association. "I think our present section set-up is terrible," he concluded.[7] Louttit himself, however, contributed to the immobility of the organization when in 1940 he turned over day-to-day activities to his secretary and went on active duty in the navy.

Perhaps the AAAP's most fundamental problem lay in its own composition. The organization had failed to erase the distinction between academicians and practitioners. While some members believed that only college professors had the time, facilities, and ability to lead the organization, others thought that a true professional group required direction from outside of academe. In 1939 the AAAP conducted a survey of applied psychologists in the United States; the results had some disturbing implications. The survey uncovered the names of over three thousand people working in applied psychology. Of those responding only 13 percent belonged to the AAAP, twice that number were in the APA, and over half belonged to no psychological group at all. In fact, only about a third of the respondents had the Ph.D. necessary for AAAP membership. The figures may have seemed paradoxical to some: a majority of AAAP members spent most of their time in college teaching, while the organization, ostensibly established to promote applied psychology, had membership requirements that disqualified over three-fifths of the country's practitioners. Just as important perhaps, over half the respondents who could meet the AAAP's academic standards preferred not to join the organization.

The survey sounded one other ominous note: the APA had twice as many applied psychologists as the AAAP. For although the older organization maintained its scholarly purposes, it had lower academic requirements for its associates. The AAAP had come into existence because the APA refused to become involved in professional issues. But even while the leaders of the APA were encouraging the formation of the new group, the depression forced them to consider the problems involved in finding nonacademic jobs for unemployed psychologists. The AAAP's continued functioning depended on its ability to maintain an exclusive realm of activity; it could not hope to withstand a challenge from the APA. Furthermore, many of the organizers of the AAAP were not completely committed to the new association and were awaiting a propitious moment to return it to the APA. And in the years before American entry into World War 2 the APA continued its movement away from purely scholarly interests.

In the late thirties the APA remained America's strongest psychological organization. The formation of new groups did not diminish its popularity. On the contrary, between 1935 and 1939 total membership rose almost 40 percent to reach over 2,500. Leaders of the AAAP and SPSSI routinely referred to the APA as the "parent organization," and they always believed their groups only supplemented the older association. The budget of the APA stayed small, but the potential for action grew as assets mounted. By the beginning of 1939 the APA had about $50,000 in the bank. The organization had the resources to finance large scale projects, although ordinary scholarly activities were unlikely to require such expenditure.

In addition to responding to the job crisis, the association was becoming increasingly concerned with the political situation in Europe. By 1938 the Nazi regime had forced a sizable number of scholars into exile, and many were making their way to the United States. The APA responded by creating the Committee on Displaced Foreign Psychologists to aid in finding jobs for the refugees. The committee had a difficult task, but it did manage to place thirty of the exiles in at least temporary work during its first year of operation. In 1938 the APA also joined other psychological organizations in opposing Vienna as the site of the Twelfth International Congress of Psychology, scheduled for 1941. Because of Austria's recent annexation to Nazi Germany, the city was deemed an inappropriate location for a scientific meeting. To some members this action suggested that the APA council and membership were beginning to see social responsibilities beyond teaching and research.

Other APA members opposed involvement in issues they considered beyond the realm of science. One APA affiliate, the Psychometric Society, tabled the anti-Nazi resolution for this reason. In 1939 the German member of the editorial board of the APA's *Psychological Abstracts* resigned because the resolution insulted his country. The resignation raised the possibility that the association, by becoming involved in politics, would end the international cooperation that was needed to produce the journal. Events soon trivialized this possibility, however: Germany invaded Poland, and international cooperation in psychology became a war casualty. Within the APA nonacademic issues would become more important than ever.

Gathering for their annual meeting only three days after the start of the conflict in Europe, many APA members felt unusually discontented in simply reading scholarly papers to one another. "The outbreak of European war was depressing," explained a correspondent for the *Psychologists League Journal*, "and one way of combating the sense of individual futility was in activity which had some relation to the social scene."[8] The APA went on record to deplore the New York legislature's elimination of psychologists at state penal institutions. It denounced the University of Colorado for allowing racial and political considerations to influence a decision not to rehire one of the founders of the SPSSI, I. Krechevsky. And it encouraged psychologists to study all aspects of American life which touched on peace and liberty. A more pugnacious and less disinterested set of resolutions had never before emerged from an APA meeting.

On professional issues, the association moved to unify and expand activities that several separate committees were already considering. It formed the Committee on Personnel, Promotion, and Public Relations, assigning it two duties. First, it was to coordinate the work of the committees on psychologists in public service, press relations, unemployment, and displaced foreign psychologists. Second, the committee was to find new ways for the APA to become involved in placing psychologists in appropriate jobs, opening new employment opportunities, and extending psychology's role in government service. A few years before, the APA would not have considered such activities to be appropriate for a scholarly society. Now no objections arose.

Although the APA's 1940 meeting lacked the fervor of its predecessor, it maintained the association's interest in professional matters. The Committee on Scientific and Professional Ethics made its first formal report. Organized two years before to look into the advisability of an ethical code for APA members, the committee now suggested six fields in which psychologists' conduct might need regulation: relations with colleagues, students, subjects, clients, the media, and the association itself. In addition, the committee reported that it had ranged beyond its stated responsibilities by dealing informally, privately, and successfully with several specific complaints. Originally set up as a temporary body, the ethics committee now gained permanent status. The APA instructed the committee to formulate an ethical code and to continue looking into specific cases of alleged misconduct. If informal means of resolution failed, the association permitted the committee to hold hearings and issue public reports.

The committee's mandate was somewhat broader than the one given to its counterpart in the AAAP, because the APA desired to regulate academic as well as professional conduct, and the ultimate weapon was more formidable since expulsion from the APA meant virtual banishment from organized psychology. The significant point, however, was that the association was making any effort at all to regulate members' conduct. What had been unthinkable only a few years before now became a permanent responsibility. The ethics committee took its duties seriously; in 1941 it uncovered such a clear case of plagiarism that it recommended that the APA Council ask for the resignation of the culprit. The council followed the recommendation, and the APA took another step toward professionalism.

An even more radical change occurred in 1941: the APA lowered the academic requirements for full membership. For almost twenty years the informal standard remained two major publications beyond the dissertation. Psychologists who could not attain this level of scholarship continued as associates; they paid dues but could not vote or hold office. During the thirties full members came to represent a self-perpetuating academic elite that ruled over an organization of lesser scholars and practitioners. In 1939 the APA contained three times as many associates (1,909) as full members (618). Deciding the time had come to consider democratizing the organization, the association appointed a committee on the constitution to propose among other things possible ways of narrowing the gap between the two classes of membership.

The committee apparently never considered simply giving the vote to associates. Instead it developed a series of alternate standards for full membership and conducted a mail ballot among full members to determine the most popular choice. Keeping the current publication requirement appealed to only a fifth of those voting. Almost two-thirds, on the other hand, favored a proposal to acknowledge nonresearch activity in psychology. It would allow associates to become full members after they had completed their doctorates, spent five years in the APA, and shown "evidence of acceptable contribution to psychology through research, teaching, administrative, or applied work on a full-time basis during this period."[9] The APA accepted this alternative at its 1941 meeting and accordingly amended its bylaws.

No one knew exactly what the new standards meant or how they would be applied. The constitution committee itself was divided on these points and offered only a few suggestions. The APA council had enough trouble evaluating scholarly output; the problems in judging an "acceptable contribution" in teaching or applied work promised to be even more difficult. Two things were certain, however. The APA would be admitting a large number of psychologists—one survey suggested as many as five hundred—to full membership. And the days were gone forever when the association could boast of the highest formal academic requirements of any national scholarly society. Fundamentally, the revision in membership standards only legitimized changes that had already occurred. Applied psychology was now too important to ignore. The new qualifications gave evidence that academicians agreed that psychology could be a profession as well as a science.

The 1941 meeting gave one other indication that the APA was moving in new directions. The association approved in principle a plan to establish a permanent central office with a salaried administrator and a full-time clerical staff. The proposal arose not from the growing scholarly needs of association members but from the desire to expand APA operations into areas of professional concern. A poll taken earlier in 1941 revealed that members hoped the extended secretariat would help in job placement, promote the expanded use of psychology, undertake public relations campaigns, and organize membership drives. The APA had begun activities in the first three of these fields on a temporary basis during the thirties; it now agreed to make such operations a permanent feature of the organization. Since details of the plan were not yet completed in 1941, the APA decided to defer final action until the following year.

Some leaders of the AAAP were displeased with events occurring within the APA. They saw the APA's growing interest in professional concerns as a response to the creation and expansion of their own organization. "There is plenty of historical evidence," C. M. Louttit observed, "that the APA gave no support to non-academic professional psychology until after the AAAP was formed and operating." Horace B. English predicted that the APA's continued "encroachment" into applied psychology would eventually produce a "rather ugly factional struggle and perhaps . . . a deep schism."[10] In the meantime the AAAP had no means to forestall the changes occurring within the APA.

If one event could symbolize the transformation of the APA and the comparative helplessness of the AAAP, it came in 1942 when the owner of the *Journal of Applied Psychology* put that publication up for sale. Without consulting the AAAP the APA began negotiations to buy the journal. No one on the APA council murmured a word of disapproval. The AAAP did not have the resources to make a counterbid, and its leaders had to settle for a face-saving gesture in which the APA selected the journal's new editor from among three candidates proposed by the AAAP.

In the years when the United States moved from depression to war, the APA deliberately and self-consciously continued on the road of professionalization. In part the leaders of the association may have been trying to head off the AAAP before the split in organized psychology became permanent. In another sense, however, encouraging the formation of the AAAP and taking an interest in professional issues were two responses to the same persistent problem. The APA was merely continuing and expanding policies already begun in the thirties. And it was acting against a backdrop of national mobilization which gave evidence that the central interests of psychology would soon shift from scholarly endeavor to applied work. Many of the organizational activities of psychologists showed a clear desire to anticipate psychology's increased and enlarged use in the years of mobilization and war.

The APA took its first steps to mobilize psychologists in 1939. In September the council, responding to the outbreak of hostilities in Europe, authorized the formation of a special committee to prepare psychology for the possibility of American involvement in the war. The committee was not to undertake specific projects but to act as a clearinghouse for information passing between psychologists and government agencies. Formed in November, the committee conducted a lively correspondence with psychologists around the country. Having only a weak mandate and no funds, however, the committee could not move directly to stimulate the government's demand for psychologists.

The committee soon ran into opposition from the AAAP, which had been working with the army for over a year. The AAAP's leaders resented the presumption of the APA in forming a committee to act for all of psychology without consulting them first. The APA council responded by reconstituting the committee as a joint operation with the AAAP. But the other groups were still left out, and the question arose whether the committee was truly national in scope. The chairman decided to enlist the support of the National Research Council's Division of Anthropology and Psychology, which some groups might find less threatening than the APA. The division agreed to sponsor a meeting of representatives of the six national organizations to coordinate plans and activities.

The meeting was held in August 1940, and delegates attended representing the APA, AAAP, SPSSI, Psychometric Society, Society of Experimental Psychologists, and Section I of the American Association for the Advancement of Science. The participants heard reports on NRC activities already under way: Walter Van Dyke Bingham discussed the work in the Adjutant General's Office, and John G. Jenkins recounted the efforts in pilot selection and training for the CAA. Then Leonard Carmichael explained the functioning of the newly organized National Roster of Scientific and Specialized Personnel, of which he was director. The major accomplishment of the meeting came when the delegates recommended that a permanent committee composed of representatives of the national societies be formed under the auspices of the NRC. The proposal won approval in all quarters, and the new Emergency Committee in Psychology held its first meeting in October.

The emergency committee adopted a passive approach to expanding the government's use of psychologists. It believed its essential task was to act on requests from government agencies rather than to initiate action itself. Two of its members got the job of generating demand for psychologists through informal contacts with influential people in the government. The committee never attempted any promotional efforts of the type that English had used in his dealings with the adjutant general. Although several subcommittees did make material contributions to the war effort, generally the work was widely diffused and poorly funded. The committee never became involved in the kind of massive programs that marked psychological activities within the military. Instead its major function came in providing a cloak of unity under which important organizational projects took place.

In May 1941 the emergency committee established the Subcommittee on the Listing of Personnel in Psychology under the chairmanship of Steuart Henderson Britt of George Washington University. The subcommittee's first assignment came on a request by General Lewis B. Hershey of the Selective Service System. He wanted a list of psychologists whom local draft boards could use to test inductees. In two months the subcommittee responded with 2,300 suitable names. The next job proved more difficult. The Adjutant General's Office desired the names of psychologists of draft age who might want to enter a new training program for personnel officers. To fill this request Britt and his colleagues sent out over thirteen hundred questionnaires and began personal correspondence with many psychologists who wanted more information about work in national defense. Meanwhile the navy and the air force began to use Britt's services in finding personnel for their own psychological programs. As 1941 wore on, the subcommittee assumed more of the functions of a placement office.

In November Britt proposed that the work of his subcommittee be continued and expanded within a central office that would serve all the country's psychologists. Aware of the APA's decision to establish a permanent secretariat, Britt suggested that the new office also could full that role for the association. The attack on Pearl Harbor added urgency to the proposal. The emergency committee sought financial support for the office and turned to the APA, which responded with an initial appropriation of $4,000. Meanwhile Carmichael arranged for office space in the Washington headquarters of the NRC. In February 1942 the Office of Psychological Personnel (OPP), with Britt as its salaried director, formally opened for business.

During its first six months in operation the OPP established itself as organized psychology's main focal point of activity. It maintained close relations with military and civilian agencies, and it placed dozens of psychologists in government jobs. Britt gave speeches at regional meetings of psychological societies and worked on a multitude of individual problems. At one point, acting as a consultant to the national roster, he successfully recommended a short-lived occupational deferment for civilian psychologists subject to the draft. Britt estimated that by the end of July the OPP had received over 3,700 letters, telegrams, phone calls, and visits about jobs, selective service status, and other concerns of the office.

The OPP continued its operations throughout the war, placing growing emphasis on public relations work and plans for the postwar period. There were a few complaints, but generally the OPP's activities met wide approval. One sign of its success was the continued strong support by the APA, which appropriated an additional $2,250 for 1942 and then $10,000 annually through 1945. The AAAP began a yearly $1,000 contribution in 1943. Both groups levied a special assessment on members to help finance these appropriations. Undoubtedly some of the general contentment of psychologists in their wartime employment and some of the overall success of military psychology can be attributed to the effectiveness of the OPP.

The OPP played another role as well. "It seems possible," Carmichael observed in 1942, "that this office may well mark the initiation of a central agency for psychologists which will have an important and growing effect upon the psychological profession in America as a whole."[11] The OPP bore a strong similarity to the extended secretariat authorized by the APA in 1941. The important difference lay in its support by other societies and its services to all psychologists regardless of affiliation. As the office continued its work, it more clearly became the prototype for a centralized agency to service all professional interests once the war had ended.

The emegency committee sponsored another project that was to become even more important for organized psychology than the OPP. In May 1941 Edgar A. Doll of the Vineland Training School in New Jersey sought the committee's approval for a conference to draw up long-range plans for psychology's future. The committee accepted the proposal, but Doll found little immediate interest in the project among other psychologists. His idea remained in abeyance until the spring of 1942 when Robert M. Yerkes, a committee member-at-large, took up the issue. Other members of the committee had no objections to the formation of a small subcommittee, headed by Yerkes, to study proposals for a planning conference. Yerkes, however, refused to head the group unless it had authority actually to arrange the conference. Further opposition then disappeared, and the committee instructed Yerkes to choose a subcommittee to work on the conference itself.

Some committee members would probably have opposed giving Yerkes this blank check if they had known the sum he would finally fill in. Nevertheless, Yerkes's long and dedicated psychological career must have inspired confidence in his good judgment. He was a pioneer in group testing, a leader in animal psychology, and an early (though not prominent) member of the SPSSI. He had a reputation as a tireless promoter and an enthusiastic committee worker. Moreover, he had a powerful sense of psychology's mission to help solve every kind of adjustment problem. Yerkes was, in short, a person who was likely to take his new responsibilities very seriously indeed.

Yerkes quickly chose six colleagues to join him on the new Subcommittee on Survey and Planning for Psychology. They were: Doll, Edwin G. Boring of Harvard, Alice I. Bryan of the School of Library Service at Columbia, Richard M. Elliott of the University of Minnesota, and Ernest R. Hilgard and Calvin P. Stone, both of Stanford. The composition of the group did not suggest that radical changes were in the offing. All the members had well-established careers, only three belonged to the AAAP, and only one was under forty. If they did finally suggest some startling innovations, their proposals would demonstrate not only Yerkes's ability to select coworkers who agreed with his general viewpoint but also the demand for action that almost all psychologists felt the war had imposed upon them. The group held its initial meeting, a week-long session at Vineland, in June, and it continued to meet every few months until the end of 1944.

Although the first meeting produced some suggestions for expanding psychological activity in the war, the major proposals concerned psychology's long-range future. The subcommittee began with the premise that applications of psychology would continue to expand. The subcommittee believed that the appropriate time had come to lay down plans for promoting and protecting psychology in its growing duties. The key to psychology's future success was its continuing professionalization. "In the new world order," the subcommittee explained, psychology's "knowledge and skills should be professionalized steadily and wisely so that its applications may keep pace with emerging human needs and demands for personal and social guidance."[12]

In addition to the usual professional issues, the subcommittee considered one question that had previously received scant attention—private practice. Many people considered the independent practitioner to be the backbone of any true profession. Most psychologists, however, worked for schools, clinics, businesses, and other institutions; few had their own practices. The subcommittee did not go so far as to indicate that it found such individualism anachronistic in a highly organized society, but it did state that welfare services would move steadily under public control and that psychologists should welcome and support this movement. "Professionalism and socialization," the subcommittee observed, "given wisdom and foresight in our planning for psychology, may proceed together."[13]

This observation did not merely try to make a virtue of a necessity. Psychologists had never taken much interest in private practice. Unlike doctors and lawyers, they had no heritage of nineteenth-century individualism, and they did not gaze longingly into a mythical past when their forebears worked free of outside interference. Nor did they see themselves locked in an endless life-and-death struggle with businesses and government. Psychologists had not begun their trade until the First World War. By then salaried employment had become the norm for most well-educated Americans. Psychologists raised no objections to a social order dominated by bureaucratic organizations. Indeed, applied psychology, with its emphasis on human adjustment, could only have found acceptance at a time when the individualism represented by private practice was ceasing to be an operating force in the lives of most Americans.

On the issue of unifying psychology the subcommittee presented some controversial suggestions. Taking as its premise the belief that the scientific and practical aspects of psychology should develop together, it saw the formation of interest groups as a dangerous splintering of psychology. Instead of going off in different directions, psychologists ought to try to work cooperatively. The subcommittee believed that psychologists needed a new national organization that would serve all their interests.

The subcommittee proposed that such an organization work on the problems of practitioners—job placement, public relations, certification, and ethical conduct—while acting as a publishing house for scholarly journals and monographs. After studying the structure of other societies, the subcommittee could not decide if the new organization should be composed of individuals, groups, or both. It did recommend, however, a large-scale operation, with the initial $25,000 budget to quadruple in ten years. The whole scheme was certainly ambitious; to the chairman of the emergency committee it seemed "visionary and impossible."[14]

Yerkes and his colleagues were not merely indulging their fantasies, however. As can be seen from the names they proposed for the new organization, they had a fairly definite plan of action in mind. Of the two possibilities one, the "American Institute of Psychology," had an innocuous ring, but the other smacked of revolution. The subcommittee suggested that the new organization might be called the "American Psychological Association." Suddenly the chimerical plan became an attempt to reorganize the APA and to push it even further down the road to professionalism. Discussion among psychologists would soon begin to focus on changing the association rather than establishing an entirely new organization.

The subcommittee proposed that the constituent societies of the emergency committee send delegates to a meeting that would lay out plans for the new organization. The suggested timetable envisioned the selection of representatives in September 1942, the intersociety convention in the following spring, and final approval by all groups in September 1943. The emergency committee accepted the plan and instructed the subcommittee to make preparations for the meeting. The committee also gave de facto sanction to reorganizing the APA by calling for a "constitutional convention," thus giving participants the responsibility of writing some kind of constitution. Meanwhile the national organizations began selecting their delegates. Few objections arose to these plans, in part because no one knew exactly what was going to happen.

One concomitant of the war may have facilitated action on the new organization. Complying with a request by the Office of Defense Transportation to curtail unnecessary travel, both the APA and AAAP canceled their regular meetings for the duration of the war. The ruling council of each group received authority to act for the whole society, with only the most momentous issues requring a mail ballot of the membership. Both associations held business meetings annually from 1942 to 1945, but for the most part only officers and some members living in the vicinity attended. In the APA psychologists who concentrated on scholarly activities found themselves watching from the sidelines while their association took on a new form. Full meetings probably would not have changed matters: the association was becoming a professional group even before the war; only a small proportion of members cared about organizational issues; and the annual business meetings never rejected recommendations by the council. In the last analysis the effort to transform the APA occurred not because of the desires of a small unrepresentative group but because the war instilled in all psychologists an imperative to act.

Reaction to the upcoming convention reflected more apprehension than opposition. Herbert Woodrow, president of the APA in 1941, thought the association had its own interest to protect. The proposed reorganization, he feared, would strengthen the weaker groups at the expense of the APA. Harriet O'Shea, chairman of the AAAP's Board of Affiliates, believed that ratification was scheduled too soon after the convention and advocated an extra year of deliberation. Hoping to postpone final action until 1944, she argued that "inasmuch as this war is being fought for democracy, it appears to me that we should be exceedingly careful to proceed democratically. . . ." In addition, O'Shea worried that members of affiliates who did not also belong to the AAAP would have no representation at the convention.[15] She was to raise the question of affiliated societies many more times in the following months.

Preparations for the convention continued, and the national organizations completed their selection of delegates. Probably very few psychologists believed a reorganization of the APA was in the offing. John E. Anderson, president of the association, labeled the proposal "so fantastic that it may break of its own weight." Carl Rogers, chairman of the AAAP's Clinical Section, thought that "a loose federation of psychological societies is about all we can hope for at this time."[16] Unsure of exactly what they would do, twenty-five representatives of nine organizations gathered in New York City at the end of May to plot the future of organized psychology.

Only two of the nine organizations represented at the convention—the APA and the AAAP—could significantly influence the future of American psychology. The other groups did have an interest in the proposed new organization, however, and the presence of their representatives lent an air of unity to the proceedings. Five of them had been formed in the depression or before: Section I of the American Association for the Advancement of Science, the Society of Experimental Psychologists, the National Institute of Psychology, the Psychometric Society, and the SPSSI. All were dedicated to research of one kind or another, although the SPSSI had a strong interest in political issues as well.

The two new groups represented minorities rather than interests. One was the Psychology Department of the American Teachers Association, the black counterpart of the National Education Association. The department, formed in 1938, concerned itself with the teaching and application of psychology in Negro institutions. Its numbers remained small, only reaching thirty-two in 1943. High standards may have prevented many of the other black psychology teachers from joining, for the department required that its members also belong to the APA. From its beginning the department tried somehow to involve the association with black institutions, but beyond a listing for the department in the association's *Year Book*, relations between the two organizations remained tenuous.

When the United States entered the war, Herman Canady, chairman of the department, volunteered his group's services to the NRC. Members would, he said, work on psychological questions concerning blacks as well as the general issues of testing and morale. Britt replied that the OPP had no requests for research in the psychology of blacks. Karl Dallenbach, chairman of the emergency committee, favored cooperation with the department, but he did not understand exactly what Canady wanted. The desire for wartime unity eventually prevailed, and the department received an invitation to send a delegate to the intersociety convention. It was yet another indication that scholarly exclusiveness was crumbling within the psychological establishment. Canady quickly accepted the invitation, undoubtedly pleased that his white colleagues would finally give some attention to the problems of black psychologists.[17]

The other new organization represented at the convention, the National Council of Women Psychologists (NCWP), had its roots in the period of mobilization. Women psychologists were anxious to join in the defense effort, but they found no place for themselves in the plans their male colleagues had formulated. Pleas and protests proved fruitless. "We were listened to sympathetically," recalled the NCWP's executive secretary, Gladys Schwesinger, "told to be good girls, and advised to wait until plans could be shaped up to include us."[18] In November 1941 a group of women in New York City began to organize, and a week after Pearl Harbor some fifty women psychologists met to form a national organization. Within six months the membership of the NCWP grew to 240.

Founded specifically to promote contributions to the war effort, the group moved into action on a number of fronts. One committee began preparing outlines that social agencies could use when arranging discussions on topics with psychological ramifications. Subjects were practical: how a working mother could keep her baby eating normally, hints for remaining calm under the strains of war, and so forth. In addition, local chapters of the NCWP offered their services in selecting women for the military, and members gave advice to the Women's Bureau in Washington, to civil defense organizations, and to other agencies. "The tension," Schwesinger observed in 1943, "which was generated through frustrated energy and eagerness to serve has found outlets in action."[19]

The NCWP could not resolve all the professional frustrations of its members. The typical woman psychologist held a less demanding job, earned a smaller salary, and received fewer honors from colleagues than did her male counterpart. Like other female white collar workers, women psychologists did not enjoy a rise in status during the war. Statistics compiled by the OPP showed a higher rate of unemployment among women psychologists in 1944 than in 1940. At the height of the war fully 14 percent of women with doctorates in psychology were out of work. On the other hand, women's place in psychology received more attention during the war than it had in all the previous fifty years combined. There was special interest in the role women psychologists would play when peace returned.

In 1943 John E. Anderson, who had just completed his term as APA president, gave the emergency committee a strange report on the postwar prospects of women psychologists. Arguing that "professional possibilities for women psychologists are limited," Anderson believed that they would confine most of their peacetime activities to work with children. Therefore, he argued, graduate schools should begin training a new kind of specialist. Almost all departments, however, continued to produce and encourage "theoretical-verbal" students who had neither the skills nor the personalities to be contented on these jobs. To solve this problem Anderson offered a modest proposal. Psychology departments should bar academically proficient women from their graduate programs, admitting instead those of "more moderate capacity" who would be happier working with children. "We must select more *doers* and fewer *verbalists*," he declared. The committee understandably ignored Anderson's report.[20]

With ideas like Anderson's floating through the higher circles of the psychological establishment, some women psychologists naturally hoped the NCWP would approach problems from a clearly feminist angle. But not all the group's members shared that hope. For example, the first president, Florence Goodenough of the University of Minnesota, opposed action that might seem to pit men against women. She argued that prejudice against women psychologists was already breaking down and that hard work would bring success to women just as it did to men. Goodenough feared the NCWP would turn women into an interest group and disqualify them from representing other organizations. She even opposed an endorsement of the Equal Rights Amendment.[21] So the NCWP's delegates to the convention carried no clear mandate and represented no consensus of opinion. The convention thus would not hear women psychologists speaking with one voice.

Most psychological organizations did not receive an invitation to the convention, because they did not have national constituencies. The APA's regional affiliates sent no delegates even though two of them had larger memberships than any of the invited groups except the AAAP and the APA itself. The thirteen state and local affiliates of the AAAP, whose combined membership was twice that of the parent organization, had to rely on the AAAP to look after their interests. There were also several large unaffiliated local groups, but they did not have concerns that required separate representation.

In the thirties one strong local group, the Psychologists League of New York City, had held a radical view of American society and psychology's proper role in it. Representatives from the league might have added a discordant note to an otherwise harmonious convention. But the league was no more. Its decline had begun in 1940 when the president, Daniel Harris, proposed that the organization condemn the Soviet attack on Finland. When put to a vote, the proposal lost overwhelmingly, and Harris, fearful that the league was branding itself an agent of the Communist party, resigned his office. In justifying the league's decision, an editorial in its *Journal* claimed no longer to see an intimate connection between psychological practice and the political structure. The league, the editorial announced, would discuss social issues only when they clearly affected professional goals.

During the period when other psychologists were mobilizing for national defense, the league urged circumspection. Concerned that psychologists were falling victim to government propaganda, it warned them in February 1941 that "they must not sacrifice their freedom of thought and of action for the petty seductions, indeed the wishful fantasies, of abundant jobs at high wages."[22] The jobs continued to multiply, however, and a new prosperity began to undercut the economic distress upon which the league had been founded. After the German assault on Russia and the Japanese attack on the United States, league members turned their attention to winning the war. In 1942 the league held its last meeting and ceased publication of its *Journal.* Thus the convention could proceed without any organized contribution from the far left. Questions would never arise about the kind of social system that would make the optimum use of psychology.

The intersociety convention met in New York City during the last three days of May 1943. Yerkes opened the initial session with a short talk on psychology's potential value in fostering the "mental development," "self-realization," and "social usefulness" of individuals. He predicted a revolution in "human nature, its controls, and expressions" that psychologists should join and promote. Psychology, he believed, could go beyond its current role in human engineering to "broader, more imaginative, and also more truly humane attempts" to enhance human values through "guidance, direction, counseling and enlightenment."[23] In the light of such a future unification took on new urgency.

The convention chairman, Edwin G. Boring, then turned the meeting toward practical considerations. The main issue, Boring believed, lay in reconciling the requirements of a central authority with the needs of interest groups. He invited the delegates to voice their grievances with the APA as presently constituted. The representatives of the Psychometric Society objected only to the way the association organized the scholarly sessions at the annual meeting. Schwesinger and Canady complained of the neglect suffered, respectively, by women and blacks. A delegate from the SPSSI reported that the members of that organization disliked the APA's undemocratic elections and strongly favored allowing associates to vote. Doll of the AAAP opposed the exclusiveness of the older association and warned that a reorganized APA could avoid the fragmentation of the past only by finding a place for emergent groups.

As the convention continued, even the delegates who had favored merely expanding the OPP came to believe that a loose federation of existing organizations would not sufficiently unify psychology. Thus there arose general approval of a plan to reorganize the APA into semiautonomous interest groups that together would represent the various aspects of both academic and applied psychology. "The Convention was ultimately forced to the conclusion," a later report stated, "that this new society could be realized only by a reconstitution of the American Psychological Association in such a way that it include within its expanded structure the functional interests and professional atmosphere of the American Association for Applied Psychology."[24] In effect the two groups would merge under the name of the APA.

The convention chose a committee of six to gather further specific recommendations and rewrite the APA bylaws. In keeping with the general tenor of the proposal, the new committee included only representatives of the APA and the AAAP. It was to have a draft ready for the September meetings of the two organizations.

Yerkes meanwhile was jubilant that the convention had proceeded so smoothly. It was, he told the emergency committee in August, "a wonderfully interesting exhibit in group cooperation" that displayed "an extraordinary degree of agreement" and that most participants found "extremely satisfactory."[25] Yerkes could not be sure, of course, that the specific reorganization proposals would bring a similarly favorable response.

The plan for reorganizing the APA, which was ready in September, changed the organization in several important ways. First, the stated purpose expanded from the advancement of psychology as a science to include its advancement as a "profession" and a "means of promoting human welfare" as well.[26] A similar statement had drawn charges of impropriety and illegality in the mid-thirties and had provided the pretext under which the APA leadership disabled the old Clinical Section. Now, however, no one objected to adding the goals of the practitioner to those of the scientist. The declaration erased any doubt that the new APA would act not only as a scholarly society but as a professional group as well.

The proposed bylaws gave the APA a central office to be managed by a salaried executive secretary with the help of a full-time staff. The office would aid in job placement, work on public relations, collect dues, provide business management for publications, and carry out routine administrative tasks. It would also perform specific duties assigned by the board of directors. Because of its large budget and full-time staff, the office would be able to move more quickly and effectively than any agency in either the APA or the AAAP. Although the proposed bylaws did not specify the location of the office, the success of the OPP spoke strongly for keeping operations in Washington even after the war ended.

The basic structure of the APA was also to undergo profound changes. No longer would the association represent a single group of psychologists; it now became a federation of divisions, each containing at least fifty members who had some common interest. An APA member could join more than one division, but he could not belong only to the association itself. The AAAP's sections would move intact to the new organization, where they would be joined by groups devoted to academic concerns. The new bylaws permitted the SPSSI and the Psychometric Society to become divisions and included provisions under which new groups might attain divisional status. Divisions would be free to set membership standards, hold elections, determine voting requirements, appoint committees, and in general conduct their business in any way not inimical to the APA itself.

The proposed bylaws forsook direct democracy for representative government. Divisions, geographical regions, and selected groups not in the APA would elect delegates to the council of representatives. The council, in turn, would choose most of the board of directors; of board members only the president and president-elect would be elected by the whole APA membership. The board would supervise the operations of the association. The annual business meeting would disappear, but at the same time the franchise in APA elections would expand to include associates. By granting the vote to its second-class citizens, the remodeled APA promised to be more responsive to the desires of all its members.

Although specific membership criteria would vary from division to division, the proposed bylaws established two basic classes of members—fellows and associates—and set down the general requirements for each. The standards followed those already operating in the APA, except that associates would need an extra year of either graduate work or pratical experience. All present APA associates and AAAP members would become associates in the new organization automatically. Clearly, the quest of many applied psychologists for more highly qualified practitioners would not be filled by the membership requirements of the new APA. Indeed, the remodeled association gave evidence of becoming more egalitarian than either the AAAP or the present APA.

The two groups received the proposed bylaws in September 1943. They approved the document in principle but delayed final ratification for a year. A joint committee was appointed to solicit further opinions, prepare mail ballots, and write the final version of the bylaws. The September meetings produced one substantive change in the proposals for remodeling the APA. The new organization received a board of affiliates to look after the interests of affiliated groups. Unlike its counterpart in the AAAP, the board included academic as well as applied groups and had no representation on the board of directors. With this alteration the joint committee published a tentative set of bylaws in the November *Psychological Bulletin* and thereby opened the proposal for debate among all psychologists.[27]

The reorganization plan drew very little criticism from within the APA. In April 1944 Edward E. Anderson of Wilson College raised a faint protest. Writing in the *Psychological Bulletin*, he complained that full members of the present association would lose all their privileges under the new scheme. Further, control of the organization would suffer needless and harmful decentralization while minority groups would gain dangerous power. The bylaws were so poorly written, he continued, that graduate students might be able to take control of the organization. Anderson doubted the reorganization would serve the best interests of psychology as a whole, and he favored postponing any decision at least until the association could hold a full business meeting.[28] Anderson's objections did not signal a popular uprising. In general APA members met the reorganization proposals with a deep silence that indicated some combination of approval and indifference.

Louder protests arose within the AAAP. In particular, some affiliated societies worried that their interest would be lost in the reorganized APA. In February 1944 the AAAP's largest affiliate, the New York state association, met to discuss the issue. The president pointed out that much professional activity—in legislation and civil service qualifications, for example—would continue on the state level no matter how the national association changed. Members complained that affiliates had no voice on the proposed council of representatives and feared that academicians would dominate the new organization. Alice I. Bryan, the executive secretary of the AAAP and one of the chief architects of the revised bylaws, presented the case for a remodeled APA. She could not overcome the many objections, however, and the New York state association refused to endorse the proposals.

More trouble came in March when Harriet O'Shea, chairman of the AAAP's Board of Affiliates, issued a list of objections to the new bylaws in a letter to officers of affiliated societies. First, she argued, the merger would thwart efforts to develop high, uniform standards for applied psychologists. Each division would set its own qualifications, and APA membership alone could not guarantee the competence of a practitioner. Further, the proposals were coming at least five years too soon. Applied psychology needed more time to establish its separate identity, and the disappearance of the AAAP would "weaken professional thinking." O'Shea believed that academicians would dominate the new organization, and since they failed to recognize the special "knowledge, skills, and attitudes" of the practitioner, they would not work for professional excellence in applied fields. They would, however, gain control of the *Journal of Consulting Psychology*. O'Shea listed other objections, concluding with the thought that no one had mentioned any disadvantages that the revised bylaws would bring to academicians.[29]

The following month Alice Bryan submitted a point-by-point rebuttal of O'Shea's objections. The reorganization proposals were coming at a propitious moment, Bryan argued, when psychologists needed to speak with a single voice to assure their maximum effectiveness in postwar social programs. Moreover, while the divisional structure in no way inhibited the development of high standards, the formation of one national organization might eliminate some confusion in the minds of potential employers. Most important, Bryan denied that academicians would rule the remodeled association. At least thirteen of the proposed nineteen initial divisions might properly fit into the current AAAP. "If either of the two large societies were to be afraid of being swallowed by the other," she observed, "it ought to be the APA, not the AAAP."[30]

The question remained unresolved. The March-April issue of the *Journal of Consulting Psychology* printed an anonymous attack on the proposed merger which left Bryan grumbling about "a rather extreme degree of editorial irresponsibility."[31] The joint AAAP-APA committee that was preparing a final version of the bylaws meanwhile decided to postpone any decision about the status of affiliates until after the new organization was established. The committee eliminated specific wording, substituting a vague but friendly pledge that the council of representatives would find ways to assist local groups that were trying to promote applied psychology. O'Shea responded with a suggestion that applied groups might create a federation to operate outside the new APA. The debate within the AAAP showed a deep distrust of the merger; in July a mail referendum on the proposed bylaws would indicate the size of this opposition.

The balloting, which both the APA and AAAP completed in August, produced something less than an overwhelming mandate. Members considered two questions. Should the organization approve the new bylaws? And if so, should it act in 1944 or wait until the end of the war? Of those voting in the AAAP about four-fifths favored the merger and slightly over two-thirds advocated immediate action. Less than half the members voted, however, so the will of the majority remained obscure. The APA registered almost identical approval rates, but the level of participation was even lower: almost two-thirds of the APA members did not return their ballots. In neither organization did the vote show unalloyed approval of the merger; on the other hand, the balloting gave even less evidence of widespread opposition. Despite the low participation rate the referendum involved more psychologists than any vote on any issue in the past. The results assured the adoption of the new bylaws at the September business meeting.

Because the AAAP's affiliated societies found no place for themselves in the remodeled APA, one pocket of potential resistance remained. Under the leadership of Harriet O'Shea the board of affiliates could easily become the focus of a new federated organization of applied groups. At its September meeting the board expressed its unhappiness with the new bylaws. Only with difficulty did Bryan and her allies dissuade the delegates from opposing the merger altogether. The board also had to consider a new chairman since O'Shea's term was ending in 1944. The committee that was ostensibly seeking a replacement recommended instead that she be continued in office. Proponents of the new bylaws quickly saw danger in that proposal and moved that the election be held as scheduled. The board failed to support O'Shea. When the motion carried, the most vocal opponent of the merger lost her position of influence, and further resistance became unlikely. The dispute had essentially concerned the type of organization that would most effectively advance the cause of professionalism. When the debate ended in a victory for proponents of the merger, only the technicalities of reorganization remained to be settled. After accepting the new bylaws unanimously the business meetings of the APA and AAAP adopted a plan that delayed final action for another year. September 1945 became the date when the remodeled association would be ready to begin full operations. The transitional year proved successful. The APA organized nineteen charter divisions, and the AAAP prepared for its orderly dissolution. The two organizations appointed joint committees to perfect the bylaws, develop a new professional journal, and find an administrator for the central office. Plans went awry in only two important matters: the problem of affiliates remained unresolved, and the Psychometric Society rejected divisional status and continued as an independent group.

In September 1945 the new board of directors assumed control of the APA, and three and a half years of hopes, doubts, and plans came to a conclusion. The board members voted to "express to Dr. R. M. Yerkes their appreciation of his initiative, vision, and persistent constructive endeavor in bringing about at this highly opportune time the merger of the various psychological organizations previously existing into a new structure of new and great potentialities for the development of the future of our Science."[32] Perhaps one or two board members also said a silent prayer that the wartime unification of psychology could sustain itself once peace returned.

The period between 1939 and 1945 witnessed an outburst of organizational activity that parallelled the expanding use of psychologists in national defense. Most of the changes benefited the practitioner. The lowering of the scholarly requirements for full APA membership, the founding of the OPP to facilitate psychologists' contribution to the war effort, the reorganizing of the APA in the hope of unifying psychology— these and other events symbolized the growing importance of the applied psychologist and marked important steps on psychology's road to professionalism. Never in the history of American psychology had so many profound organizational changes occurred so rapidly.

In one sense, the events of the wartime period merely continued trends of the thirties when applied psychologists had organized in earnest and the APA had become involved in promoting nonacademic jobs. Interest in professional issues had grown steadily throughout the decade and expanded further after 1939. Meanwhile the attempt to resolve the perennial conflict between academicians and practitioners by establishing separate organizations for each did not prove to be satisfactory to either group. The renovation of the APA signaled but another approach to a problem that had plagued psychologists for thirty years. No one would deny the effect of the war, however. It stimulated and channeled organizational activity in ways that few psychologists could have predicted in 1938.

The war produced an unparalleled demand for work on practical psychological problems. The government bestowed on psychologists a new social purpose, the fulfillment of which depended in part on effective organization. The creation of the OPP and the transformation of the APA represented constructive efforts of psychologists to mobilize themselves for public service. An element of self-aggrandizement was undoubtedly also involved, for psychologists realized that successful work in the war effort would greatly enhance their status. Nevertheless, during World War 2 professionalism, unity, and patriotism were more thoroughly intertwined than at any other time.

In addition to new feelings of self-importance, the war promoted other attitude changes among psychologists. Many of the academicians who took applied jobs found their sense of alienation from practitioners diminishing. The distinctions that had meant so much before the war faded into triviality when seen against the backdrop of the great national struggle then under way. More than ever before psychologists saw themselves as a single group rather than a jumble of competing factions. With the new feelings of importance and unity came apprehension that prewar conditions might return. Organizational deliberations assumed an unusual air of urgency, and circumspection gave way to decisive action. The stakes were high. The leaders of organized psychology realized that only by institutionalizing wartime gains would psychologists become prepared to seize peacetime opportunities.

The remodeled APA promised major benefits to practitioners. It made applied psychologists an intrinsic part of one inclusive, national organization. They were no longer the unwanted appendages of a scholarly group, and they could speak to clients and employers in the name of all American psychology. The organization would permit effective action on professional issues. As clearer channels of communication opened between practitioners and the designers of graduate curricula, for example, the chances for standardized training programs would grow appreciably. In addition, an ethical code backed by the prestige of the APA would have real coercive power, for expulsion from the association amounted to ostracism from organized psychology. Self-certification might now prove effective for much the same reaason, especially if the new central office could develop public relations campaigns that successfully explained the differences between genuine psychology and attractive imitations. Of critical importance was the willingness of the remodeled association to mobilize resources to carry through its programs; its initial annual budget totaled twice the prewar expenditure of the APA and AAAP combined.

Applied psychology had reached a kind of "takeoff point" on the journey to professionalism. After years of effort applied psychologists had rid themselves of the most burdensome internal and external impediments to rapid professionalization. Now as never before they were free to move as far as their skills would carry them down the road to professional status. Of course, no one knew in 1945 how successful the renovated APA would become in attacking professional issues. Practitioners had no guarantees that their academic colleagues would provide needed support; wartime unity might fade quickly and completely. Moreover, professionalization depended in large measure on factors only partly in the control of psychologists themselves. Growing popular interest, continuing government support, and declining opposition from psychiatrists and other groups all would play crucial roles. Nevertheless, practitioners had far more command of their destiny in 1945 than at any time in the past. They faced an unprecedented demand for their services, and they enjoyed a newly won equality within the APA. A leading aviation psychologist found the appropriate metaphor to describe the recent changes. "During World War 2," he declared, "the profession of psychology came of age."[33]

7

APPLIED PSYCHOLOGY
IN THE POSTWAR ERA

As the curtain rose, ten young cadets stood facing the mechanical testing apparatus. The examiner told them to be seated and gave them their
instructions. Each cadet was to grasp the rod in front of him and hold
it so steadily that it did not touch the sides of the metal aperture sur-
rounding it. A light would flash every time a cadet made an error by
allowing the rod to bump its enclosure. Each cadet was required to keep
an accurate count of his mistakes. Before beginning the test the examiner
explained that its purpose went far beyond simply gauging muscle control:

The test that you are to take now will measure your ability to remain
steady under pressure. The pressure will consist of your anxiety to succeed
in Air-Crew training. It will consist of your own fear that you will be
eliminated. It will consist of your own weakness and secret doubts. It will
consist of jumping nerves that you cannot control.
This test will pit you against yourself. Every man has fear. Every man
has tenseness. Every man has weakness and jumping nerves and secret
doubts. But not every man can control these things.

Then the first trial began. For ten seconds the cadets tried to keep their
arms steady, but the lights continued to flash. Tension mounted as the
examiner reminded the cadets that each mistake brought them closer to
failure. There were four more trials exactly like the first. Then the test
was over. The stage lights faded, and the curtain fell.[1]
This scene, probably the first ever to depict the dramatic aspects of
psychological testing, marked the high point in Moss Hart's semidocumen-
tary Broadway play of 1943, *Winged Victory*. One critic declared that
"the scene in which the cadets are undergoing the steadiness-under-

pressure test, the test of the winking lights, is an ordeal for every person in the audience, and I doubt if many passed."[2] A year later, when Hollywood made a film version of the play, all Americans got a chance to agonize with the young cadets who were trying to overcome the diabolical challenge to their competence and self-esteem.

It may not be too far-fetched to suggest that the testing scene from *Winged Victory* marked the point at which applied psychology became serious business for the American public. The scene's message was clear: everyone had a realm within his personality that lay beyond his immediate understanding and control. The requirements of a technological society, however, demanded that each person mobilize his innermost resources. No one could be spared a probing of his "weaknesses and jumping nerves and secret doubts" if social needs were to be met effectively. The scene, in short, made a striking case for the necessity not only of adjustment itself but of sophisticated methods to achieve it. The scene did not invite skepticism, although some was warranted. Even before the play opened, air force psychologists had abandoned an improved version of the steadiness-under-pressure test, determining that it had not proved effective in predicting which cadets would succeed in aviation training.

The scene from *Winged Victory* heralded an era in which psychology came to have a greater impact on the American consciousness than it ever had before. In the period after World War 2 movies, books, and magazines would grow less satisfied with moral or sociological explanations and would turn to psychological interpretations of human behavior. Characters, whether real or fictional, would appear more fascinating when their psyches were opened for public examination. Psychology would, however, provide more than mere diversion and amusement. It would also become a large-scale enterprise, and the public would pour countless millions of tax dollars into psychological research and training. One of the chief beneficiaries of the great popular fascination with psychology would be the psychologists themselves: as people concerned themselves increasingly with the psychological aspects of living and working, the demand for psychological services would reach unprecedented dimensions.

The movies were one area of popular culture in which the war marked the beginnings of a trend toward broadly psychological themes. Films about psychology had emerged in the 1920s, observes film critic Leslie Halliwell, but "the subject took its firmest hold in the middle of World War 2. . . ."[3] Characters suffering from various mental derangements appeared with increasing frequency. Beginning with sexual repression in *Lady in the Dark* (1944), audiences examined a full range of cases from amnesia (as in *Spellbound* with its surrealistic dream sequences) to homicidal schizophrenia (as in *The Dark Mirror*). Maladjusted protagonists soon became familiar figures on the silver screen—and later on the television tube as well.

Applied psychologists received only secondhand benefits from these films, however, for the psychotherapists depicted in them were almost always psychiatrists. Psychologists could not view a movie about themselves until 1952, when Stanley Kramer produced *My Six Convicts.* The story concerned a psychologist's efforts to set up a testing program in a federal penitentiary. Although the plot lacked the unpredictable twists of the usual psychological melodrama, it maintained interest by describing the growing friendship between the psychologist and the prisoners who worked for him. The film downplayed the importance of the psychologist's research and emphasized his ability to foster trust and self-esteem in the prisoners. While audiences gained only a vague notion of what psychological work entailed, they could easily have concluded that psychologists were sympathetic people with a deep faith in the decency of their fellow men.

Generally psychological themes carried an element of mystery and even insidiousness. This proved especially true in the realm of social criticism. Through the 1950s, at least, critiques of American society became analyses of the American psyche. The titles alone told of psychological troubles: *The Lonely Crowd, The Organization Man, The Hidden Persuaders.*

Further evidence of the nation's psychological degeneration seemed to come from Korea, where American prisoners of war fell victim to something called "brainwashing." It was a sign of the times that Americans discounted duress and conversion in seeking an explanation of the prisoners' behavior. They saw instead, in the words of *Life* magazine, "an effort, as finely organized as any battle plan, to capture the minds of American prisoners. . . ."[4]

By the early sixties America's preoccupation with psychic deficiencies had begun to give way to a new interest in social problems. War, poverty, racism, and other issues became topics of public concern and scholarly inquiry. Psychologists did not suffer from the seeming deemphasis of personal problems, however, for each social issue had psychological ramifications. The prime example came in the struggle for civil rights, where psychological testimony on the deleterious effects of segregation influenced both the courts and the public. By the late sixties social protest came increasingly from college campuses, where demands for societal change mixed with the more personal goals of "relevance" and "doing your own thing." Psychology courses enjoyed unprecedented popularity; among established disciplines only anthropology showed a higher rate of increase in college majors.

Further evidence that interest in psychology did not decline in the late sixties came in the growing success of the popular monthly *Psychology Today*. Founded in 1967, the magazine offered simplified accounts of behavioral research in an illustrated slick-paper format. Bona fide psychologists, psychiatrists, and other experts wrote most of the major articles. Unlike its predecessors of thirty years before, *Psychology Today* aimed at a well-educated audience that did not seek facile advice on successful living. Though not a scholarly journal, the magazine did provide reliable information on the psychological aspects of important topics. Its popularity may be measured by its circulation, which had soared beyond 900,000 by 1974.

At the same time Americans continued their long-standing quest for a more satisfying life. Advocates of pseudoscientific or quasi-religious approaches still had their followers, of course, but to an increasing extent people turned to genuine psychologists for advice. Readers of paperbacks, for example, could catch the latest word from notables like Erich Fromm, learn about the newest therapeutic techniques ("reality therapy," "scream therapy," etc.), or discover how to renew self-esteem in books with snappy titles like *I Ain't Much Baby but I'm All I've Got.* The electronic media had their psychologists too, led by Joyce Brothers, the ebullient former quiz-show winner who had become something of a national celebrity by the mid-seventies.

Although postwar interest in psychology had some aspects of a popular fad, it also received strong backing from the federal government. The contacts that psychologists had made with federal agencies did not fade as had happened after World War 1. Instead, military programs continued on a reduced scale, and the Office of Naval Research provided funding for basic research in psychology as well as other sciences. Postwar aid, especially for clinical psychology, came from the Veterans Administration and the Public Health Service. While psychologists received only about 1 percent of the government's science dollar, the level of financing still dwarfed prewar figures. In the thirty years after World War 2, the federal government spent over $1.2 billion on psychological research. By 1972 over half the members of the American Psychological Association were receiving government subsidies for their work.

The availability of federal funding encouraged many students to pursue advanced degrees in psychology. The decade following the end of the war saw a striking growth in the number of doctoral recipients. In 1955 American universities granted almost one-tenth of their doctorates in the field of psychology. That proportion dropped in subsequent years, but after a slump in the late fifties the absolute figures for Ph.D.s in psychology rose sharply, reaching 2,400 by 1973. The economic recession of the seventies did somewhat decrease the popularity of doctoral programs. Nevertheless, graduate students could still pursue the Ph.D. with strong assurance that they—unlike their counterparts in other disciplines—would be able to find appropriate jobs after the completion of their study and training. Psychologists could count on a continuing interest in their field and a strong demand for their services. APA membership statistics provided one source of confidence: in the thirty years after the end of the war the number of association members increased tenfold. Opportunities for new psychologists arose in all specialties. Sizable college enrollments and generous federal grants kept academic psychology in good health and stimulated thousands of new jobs on college faculties. But even more than teachers and researchers the public wanted practitioners—experts who could help individuals with personal problems and aid administrators in the efficient management of students and employees. School officials, businessmen—even psychiatrists—turned to applied psychologists in growing numbers after World War 2. As American society grew more complex, the need for expert assistance in adjustment became more acute. By the early fifties the need for applied psychologists had grown so large that practitioners outnumbered academicians for the first time. The three major fields of applied work—industrial, educational, and clinical—each enjoyed unprecedented prosperity in the postwar era.

The postwar growth of industrial psychology had its roots in events that occurred during the war. The military had given psychologists a chance to prove the effectiveness of selection, classification, and aptitude testing, and psychologists met the challenge successfully. Civilian employers also offered new opportunities, which grew largely from the labor shortage produced by wartime mobilization. Business managers, beset by high rates of absenteeism and job turnover, took unprecedented interest in hiring the right worker and keeping him contented on the job. Management turned to psychologists and other behavioral scientists for help, and the amount of psychological testing quickly increased. Surveys showed that in 1939 only 14 percent of businesses were using such tests; in 1947 the proportion rose to 50 percent, and in 1952, 75 percent.[5] Industrial psychologists believed that they had a greater contribution to make than simply producing more and better tests. They increasingly joined teams of experts from other fields whose members could attack complex problems from a number of angles. Psychologists expanded their involvement in engineering, where their duties focused on analyzing the "human factors" of "man-machine interaction." They aided, for example, in designing aircraft cockpits and space capsules. Meanwhile other psychologists applied the principles of social psychology to help businesses increase sales through market research, advertising, and public relations. The "hidden persuaders" thus counted psychologists among their number.

The APA recongized the diversifying interests of industrial psychologists by establishing separate divisons of engineering and consumer psychology. The primary work of industrial psychologists centered within the business organization itself. The essential problem remained as it had since the twenties—how to raise efficiency and increase profits—but the focus of attention shifted from the individual worker to the relationships between workers, and the new topics of concern came from social psychology rather than test-construction. Psychologists joined sociologists and other experts to study the norms and goals of work groups, conflicts within management, communications between employees, and other questions arising from the business's organizational structure. To reflect these new problems and responsibilities, industrial psychologists gave their field a new name, "organizational psychology," which quickly caught on with those who wanted to break away from the limitations of the past.

The changes within industrial psychology had mixed effects on professional development. The great postwar demand stimulated full-time work in the field. The typical pattern of the twenties and thirties—an academic psychologist "moonlighting" as a consultant to a local business firm—faded as industrial psychologists abandoned academic ties and accepted jobs directly with businesses, government, or private consulting firms. On the other hand, the "systems approach," which called upon experts from several fields, diminished the psychologist's realm of exclusive competence. Industrial psychologists could not, for example, successfully claim to provide more reliable advice on group norms or public opinion than industrial sociologists, who had shown a professional interest in these fields at least since the Hawthorne studies of the late twenties.

The postwar decades witnessed increasing criticism of industrial psychology. William H. Whyte argued that personality tests were helping to produce "organization men" by weeding out prospective executives whose psychic characteristics deviated from company norms. Whyte saw private enterprise becoming mired in conformity; as an antidote he included in his book a short explanation on how to "cheat" on personality tests.[6] Loren Baritz attacked an even more vulnerable point in his historical account *The Servants of Power* (1960). He contended that psychologists and other behavioral scientists had put themselves at the disposal of the managerial elite. Their work reflected the needs of management—for greater productivity, less conflict with workers, and higher profits—while denying that labor had any legitimate interests of its own.

Essentially Baritz presented the piper-and-tune dilemma faced by all professionals who are hired by one group but practice on another. To sustain its existence, applied psychology needed to provide a marketable service that administrators could use for their own purposes. Yet psychologists who acted merely as technicians had a weak claim to professional status. In this situation the poorly adjusted psychologist who found that scientific objectivity conflicted with the values of his employer had either to resolve the conflict or find more congenial work. The usual form of resolution posited a harmony of interest among those concerned, so that the personal goals of workers, students, and patients complemented the institutional aims of businesses, schools, and hospitals. Industrial psychologists met special problems here because many workers had joined unions and saw labor and management in perpetual conflict over wages, working conditions, and similar issues. Especially in the sixties, though, psychologists working in schools and clinics also discovered that they based their operations on values that were not accepted by all groups in society.

The Second World War affected educational psychology less markedly than it did the other applied fields. Psychological testing had firmly established itself in the schools before the war, and psychologists played only a small direct role in the military's educational programs. Nevertheless the postwar changes in educational psychology did have some wartime roots. Mobilization promoted a professional consciousness among many school psychologists who had previously been concerned largely with local issues. Not only did they have an opportunity to work with other psychologists in a new setting, but they also became a prime target of the APA's wartime membership drive. When the association reorganized in 1945-46, it established a separate division of school psychologists distinct from the division of educational psychology that had been carried over from the AAAP.

The founding of the two divisions marked a lasting split in psychologists who were involved with educational problems. "Educational psychology" came to refer largely to an academic specialty concerned with research in the various aspects of learning. "School psychology" became the name for the field that applied psychological knowledge to specific problems in individual schools. The new distinction was logical and practical, and it facilitated the practitioners' drive for professional status by detaching them from the academicians. Later in the postwar period school psychology added a new dimension with implications similar to those of organizational psychology in the industrial field. Some school psychologists found themselves responsible for improving morale among teachers and pupils, studying groups that influenced school policies, recommending reforms in the curriculum, and generally trying to view the school as a "system."

Another new function for school psychologists came as a result of wartime experiences. The war had focused public attention on mental health, and many psychologists had become involved in clinical work. After the war some school psychologists added psychotherapy to the list of services they provided. Some colleagues voiced criticism of this trend, arguing that school psychologists could not afford to spend such time and effort on a single child and that school psychologists lacked sufficient education and training—most only had master's degrees—to practice successfully. Brief, informal counseling from a psychotherapeutic viewpoint drew less opposition, however, especially when the community did not provide alternate facilities for treating poorly adjusted children. The amount of therapy that school psychologists did was thus partly a matter of definition. At any rate, individual counseling or "systems approaches" seldom preempted the school psychologist's traditional duties.

Testing remained the school psychologist's most frequent task. With the growth of special education classes teachers referred an increasing number of students to the psychologist for individual testing of intelligence, learning disabilities, and personality. In addition, school psychologists often aided in choosing, administering, and interpreting standardized group tests. Beyond testing, duties included consultation with teachers, nontherapeutic counseling of students, and a wide variety of other tasks. The exact nature of the psychologist's responsibilities depended less on his education and training than on the desires of school administrators and the availability of other specialists, but both these groups threatened the school psychologist's claim to professional status—the administrators by restricting his independence and the other specialists by challenging his exclusive competence in fields such as pupil guidance and special education.

It was testing that secured the psychologist's position in the school and stimulated the continued growth of school psychology. Beginning in the sixties, however, intelligence testing came under increasingly bitter attack from minority groups, social commentators, and some psychologists. They complained that I.Q. scores measured only a minor aspect of intellectual ability and that test items reflected middle class values and experiences. Because the lower class contained a disproportionate number of racial minorities, it followed that the intelligence test acted ultimately as a tool of oppression. The assault on the I.Q. received a wide public hearing. One television network even presented an hour-long exposé called "The I.Q. Myth," in which intelligence tests received an unmitigated denunciation.

The I.Q. came under a cloud of suspicion, but the cloud had a silver lining. The telecast, for example, found that individual tests were more valid than those given to groups, that special intelligence tests could be constructed for cultural minorities, and that aptitude tests were largely free of racial bias. Indeed, viewers might have concluded not that the intelligence test should be abolished but rather that it ought to be supplemented by tests to measure creativity, diagnostic ability, and other intellectual qualities. Schools, of course, could not yet make use of such scores, but the quest for administrative efficiency hardly precluded such a possibility in the future. If the answer to the shortcomings of the I.Q. tests turned out to be other tests, then school psychologists could count on an important and growing role in the educational system for years to come.

Of the three applied fields clinical psychology underwent the most changes in the postwar period. Military needs in the last years of the war had pulled large number of psychologists into clinical work. When the war ended, the Veterans Administration found itself with 44,000 neuropsychiatric patients and only a few clinical psychologists. In 1946 it established a program of subsidies and internships for graduate students in clinical psychology with the hope of greatly increasing America's supply of clinicians in only a few years. This ambitious program proved extremely successful. Responding to a growing demand, largely from the VA and other public agencies, graduate schools began producing more Ph.D.s in the clinical field than in any other specialty. Much to the chagrin of many academicians, this trend continued throughout the postwar period. In 1973, for example, graduate departments awarded nearly 40 percent of their Ph.Ds to specialists in clinical or counseling psychology.

Their growing numbers meant added strength for clinical psychologists in the perennial struggles with charlatans, psychiatrists, and academicians. Other consequences of the war also enhanced the prospects for professionalism. Experience in the VA hospitals gave clinical psychologists an unprecedented opportunity to work with adults. Interest in children remained strong, but the child guidance clinic ceased to be the major employer of clinicians. Clinical psychology thus widened its clientele and lost some of its "nurturative" orientation. At the same time postwar educational subsidies such as the G.I. bill brought a disproportionate number of men to college campuses. The percentage of women in clinical programs declined accordingly. Membership in national organizations reflected the change: in 1941 women composed 43 percent of the AAAP's clinical section; thirty years later the equivalent division in the APA contained less than 20 percent women. No longer could anyone dismiss clinical psychology as "not man's work," for men were practitioners in overwhelming numbers. The clinicians' quest for professionalism could thus continue without requiring a simultaneous advance in the status of women. The clearest sign of professionalism in the clinical setting was the performance of psychotherapy. During the war psychiatrists abandoned their claim to exclusive rights in this field, falling back to the position that they must only have overall supervision of psychiatric patients. After the war the number of cases—in hospitals, community clinics, and other medical facilities—remained far beyond the treatment capability of psychiatrists alone. They thus supported government subsidization of clinical psychology, though perhaps with some foreboding. In the postwar period the psychiatrist still ran the clinical team, but the roles of its members became more ambiguous than ever before. Meanwhile the number of strictly psychological clinics continued to grow, and a small but significant proportion of clinical psychologists took up private or group practice. In both these settings the clinicians could engage in psychotherapy without even the nominal control of a psychiatrist.

The growing acceptance of psychologists in therapy stemmed to some extent from the variety of techniques they offered. While psychiatrists were trying strenuously to protect traditional psychoanalysis from nonmedical practitioners, clinical psychologists not only continued to develop the methods they had used during the war, but they later pioneered striking new approaches to psychotherapy as well. For the handicapped, clinicians offered counseling designed to help the patient discover and use the personal resources he still had available. Group therapy became very popular; it stretched the service of the therapist while lowering costs to the patient. In individual treatment some clinical psychologists continued with one or another version of psychoanalysis, but many others turned to the nondirective "insight therapy" of Carl Rogers, which tried to summon the client's own resources to overcome his problems. For over a decade this technique furnished clinical psychology's main claim to an original, non-Freudian approach in psychotherapy.

In the sixties traditional psychotherapy received two serious but widely differing challenges. One was behavior modification, a system that derived from the principles of John B. Watson and his most energetic postwar disciple, B. F. Skinner. It involved "applying experimentally established laws and paradigms of learning to overcoming unadaptive habits in human beings."[7] Assuming that maladjusted people could be treated like laboratory animals, this approach took no interest in conscious or subconscious mental states and instead concentrated entirely on changing behavior. Because it relied on the therapist's ability to control the environment, behavior modification achieved its greatest popularity in institutions such as prisons and mental hospitals where the recipients had little say about what happened to them. The system quickly aroused controversy, not only among psychologists who objected to its theoretical premises but also among civil libertarians who feared its overt authoritarianism. The other challenge to traditional psychotherapy came from "humanistic psychology," a term used by Abraham H. Maslow and others who doubted that people should be used as objects of scientific inquiry. More protesters than systematizers, the "humanists" became associated with a wide variety of developments. Especially important were sensitivity groups in which participants sought "self-actualization" through "altered states of consciousness." Existentialism, Eastern mysticism, and equipment to measure brainwaves all became part of humanistic psychology, which an article in *Psychology Today* in 1972 proclaimed as "the erratic heart of the counterculture."[8] This was not the position that many psychologists envisioned for themselves, and they thus believed that "humanism" threatened both their science and their profession. Nevertheless, the movement promised to broaden psychology's clientele considerably. Its ideas and techniques attracted members of the middle class who, rather than showing clear signs of maladjustment, experienced only vague feelings of discontent that had previously been outside the purview of clinical work.

In some ways behavior modification and humanistic psychology represented the two alternative identities assumed by clinical psychology in the postwar period. In one guise the clinician was a scientist who retained a strong interest in research and hoped to discover valid generalizations about human thought and behavior. In the other he was an artist and technician who took special interest in the unique aspects of each case and found research largely irrelevant to helping individuals achieve better adjusted lives. A planning conference of clinical psychologists recommended in 1949 that graduate training include preparation for both service and research. This divided focus, which characterized postwar doctoral programs, never had total support among clinical psychologists, and it received increasing criticism as opportunities for therapy expanded. Another conference in 1973 recommended that graduate departments recognize that research had become an optional aspect of the clinician's role and change their programs accordingly. This proposal, if widely implemented, would take clinical psychology another step away from scholarship and toward professionalism.

In trying to define their identity clinical psychologists had to face a number of severe criticisms. One objection focused on the notion that mental illness was merely a contemporary label for social deviance. Through diagnosis and treatment, the argument ran, clinical psychologists promoted and justified the ostracism or repression of individuals who did not adhere to the dominant values of American society. Like other applied psychologists, clinicians were told that they failed to understand the social implications of their work. Other critics questioned the effectiveness of psychotherapy. Beginning in the fifties, a number of studies seemed to demonstrate that patients treated by psychologists or psychiatrists showed no more improvement than those who had not received any treatment at all. Clinicians appeared to be doing better for themselves than for their clients. Thus there arose in some minds the picture of a clinical psychologist who had no interest in research and doubtful competence in practice and whose main task was defending the status quo.

Many clinical psychologists believed that the answer to these criticisms lay in "community psychology." Using this approach, clinicians would promote personal adjustment not by treating individuals but by influencing policy makers who could produce changes in the community's institutions. One text, for example, in listing priorities for clinical psychology in 1973, declared that "of highest importance is the design and development of public programs for psychological well-being."[9] Therapy might then be turned over to empathetic subordinates whose personal qualities made up for a lack of extensive formal training in clinical work. Under this scheme, clinical psychologists would spend their time in planning and supervising. Thus clinicians would need to be neither scientists nor practitioners; they could become administrators. Whatever other benefits community psychology might bring, it at least promised to create a layer of ancillary workers such as already existed in many professions.

The American Psychological Association emerged from the war with a great potential for promoting applied psychology. The APA had the authority and the resources to move effectively on standardized training, certification, ethical behavior, and other professional issues. But the organization was still split between practitioners and academicians, and some applied psychologists wondered whether it could develop the will to act. If the association's leaders had waited for a consensus on all issues, the organization probably would have stagnated; instead they tried to move in a variety of directions at once, providing benefits to both halves of the membership. This policy left no one entirely happy, but it nevertheless kept the APA a strong and effective organization in its dealings with groups outside psychology. The association increasingly took on the duties of a professional organization, but it never abandoned the needs of the academicians in its ranks.

The postwar era saw profound changes in the APA. They came not so much in general policy and direction—for these had been largely determined during the war—as in the size and scope of its operations and the mood and interests of its members. The membership of the APA grew from about 4,000 in 1945 to some 40,000 thirty years later. The annual budget showed an even greater increase, rising from $100,000 at the end of the war to more than $7 million in the midseventies. The size of the central office also expanded: Britt's shoestring operation during the war burgeoned into a minor bureaucracy of 160, and a few desks provided by the National Research Council became a multimillion-dollar edifice in downtown Washington. The association's activities grew so extensive and so diverse that in 1970 it established a monthly newspaper, the *APA Monitor*, to keep members informed about what it was doing.

The membership itself changed in ways not entirely explained by the numerical preponderance of practitioners over academicians. Psychologists in all fields enjoyed a growing prosperity, and the somber asceticism of the prewar years disappeared for all those who did not desire it. Being a psychologist somehow became more fun. The *APA Monitor* published cartoons, avoided technical reports, and often assumed an irreverent attitude toward what were ostensibly burning controversies. The annual meetings moved off college campuses and into convention cities like New Orleans and Honolulu. The caliber of papers seemed to decline, while the many exhibits produced what the *Monitor* called "a carnival atmosphere."[10] At the New Orleans meeting in 1974, for example, the stellar attractions were how-to-do-it sex films, which drew standing-room-only crowds.

The APA reflected its members' more sober interests as well. Most psychologists had a personal stake in national science and mental health policy; they kept their eyes on the federal budget and their minds on possible grant proposals. Representing these interests, the APA led the drive for federal funding with a well-organized lobbying effort in Washington. Unlike the prewar period, this era saw psychologists moving confidently on Capitol Hill and among the administrative agencies. They did not act merely in their own interests, of course, since federal officials needed guidance on how to organize the many new research and training programs in psychology. The APA also rendered the government other assistance. For example, the association came to the aid of the Central Intelligence Agency. Because of the covert nature of its work, the CIA could not publicly acknowledge this assistance, but in 1951 it did privately thank the APA for help in, among other things, recruiting "qualified and competent psychologists for Agency employment."[11] Such secrecy was exceptional, and for the most part the association's connections with the government remained aboveboard and open to the scrutiny of its members.

The government hastened the APA's action on one important professional issue, the development of standardized training programs. In

1945 the leaders of the Veterans Administration were planning to subsidize training in clinical psychology and other mental health fields. They first contacted the navy's chief clinical psychologist, who found them someone to help set up the program in clinical psychology. They then went to the APA to request a list of graduate schools capable of providing the desired training. A quick response was essential, for the VA hoped to begin the program in the fall of 1946. Within a few months a committee of the association examined the programs and facilities of the nation's psychology departments and submitted the names of those suitably qualified. The APA thus became an accreditation agency for graduate programs in clinical psychology, a function it later assumed for other applied fields as well. The VA's request provided a test case for the reorganized APA; the association's response showed that the organization would move decisively on professional issues.

The APA did not attempt to use its new accrediting powers to enforce homogeneity in graduate programs. In clinical psychology it demanded instead only course offerings in certain fields, a year of internship, and a doctoral dissertation. Each department designed its own program within these guidelines, in part because the APA believed there was strength in diversity and in part because academics resented outside interference in their departments. The association did, however, insist on original research as part of the doctoral requirements, a position that drew increasing criticism among practitioners.

In 1968 the psychology department at the University of Illinois acted to answer the critics. Without abandoning the Ph.D. for students who had an interest in research, it inaugurated a new program that replaced the dissertation with further practical training and led to the doctor of psychology (Psy.D.) degree. Applied psychologists had been talking about this idea for at least thirty years, and they now waited to see how it would work in practice. The early results were favorable. Students of the Psy.D. program did well academically, and they found jobs easily once prospective employers understood the nature of the new degree. In 1973 the APA accredited the program at the University of Illinois, and a planning conference for clinical psychology endorsed the Psy.D. as an alternative to the traditional doctorate. With the new degree, applied psychology took an important, although still tentative, step away from its academic origins. Like physicians and lawyers, applied psychologists now had their own doctorate, an unambiguously professional degree untainted with any element of useless scholarship.

The APA accompanied the accreditation of graduate programs with its first effort at individual certification since the twenties. In 1946 the association established a national certifying agency, the American Board of Examiners in Professional Psychology, to issue diplomas in several applied fields. This scheme resembled that of twenty years before, except that it included the passing of a formal examination as well as the possession of the requisite amounts of training and experience. Although the diploma might have impressed some psychologists, it did not seem necessary to most clients and employers. Graduate degrees alone became the admission tickets to psychological practice. Although certification may have been helpful in specific cases, the scheme lacked both legal and moral force, and generally the psychologists who earned diplomas were exactly the ones whose unusually high qualifications needed no special recognition. Judged by the participation rate—by 1973 less than 7 percent of APA members—the new program proved only a bit more successful than the abortive attempt at national certification in the twenties.

Meanwhile the struggle for legal certification continued in many states. Before the war applied psychologists had debated the desirability and possibility of obtaining legislative sanction for their activities. In the postwar era state associations grew in number, and like the APA, they increased their members, resources, and influence. They could thus make a more powerful case to state legislatures than ever before. The organized opposition to the principle of certification by psychiatrists and other physicians diminished, and applied psychologists were able to compromise their differences with the medical profession. Beginning in 1945, when Connecticut passed the first certification law, state associations enjoyed three decades of legislative success. States not only enacted laws limiting the title "psychologist" to qualified practitioners, but many went further, and after exempting physicians and sometimes clergymen from the provisions of the law, they defined the specific duties that psychologists could exclusively perform. The laws usually required the psychologist to possess a doctorate and sometimes to take an examination or have one or more years' experience. By the mid-seventies all but four states had passed certification laws of some kind.

During the war some practitioners had feared that the reorganized APA would ignore certification and other issues requiring action on the state level. The failure of the new bylaws to provide for affiliated societies had left some room for legitimate doubt, but the APA quickly moved to settle the question by establishing the Conference of State Psychological Associations. This group sent representatives to the APA Council and generally resembled the AAAP's old Board of Affiliates. Its influence helped to keep the national organization involved in state affairs. In 1959, for example, the APA agreed to provide grants and interest-free loans to state associations that were embroiled in legislative struggles but had exhausted their own resources.

Applied psychologists had long believed that, while certification and standardized training would insure general competence, only a binding ethical code could guarantee professional conduct. In the years before American entry into the war, the APA had taken an important step in this direction by establishing a committee to oversee the behavior of its members. In 1947 the association went further and began work on a formal set of principles. Attempting to base standards on current practice, a committee polled APA members to discover how they had handled their ethical problems. This approach, which seemed to equate custom with morality, assured that the formulated principles would gain wide support among practitioners. As finally drafted, the code required psychologists to recognize their own limitations, protect the interests of their clients, maintain the integrity of tests and other instruments, and live up to the social responsibilities that psychological practice entailed.

The APA adopted the code in 1952 and revised it periodically thereafter. Although the association's ethics committee continued to operate informally in dealing with alleged misconduct among members, the code at least provided a recognized standard by which behavior could be judged. Moreover, state certification laws sometimes mentioned the code in defining the ethical requirements of psychological practice. In 1972 the APA, anticipating the concern of the federal government, took another step in regulating the conduct of its members by developing a new code to govern the use of human subjects in research. Psychologists did not place complete faith in their codes, however, and in 1955 the APA arranged for malpractice insurance to be offered to its members. This protection was not merely one of the trappings of professionalism, as a clinical psychologist from California may have discovered in 1972 when he lost a $170,000 malpractice suit.

During the postwar years applied psychologists determined that professional status could help them earn very attractive incomes. Thus the perennial rift between practitioners holding doctorates and those with only master's degrees became in part a struggle for jobs and financial well-being. In 1957 the APA, dominated as it was by Ph.D.s, drew back from the egalitarianism of the war and established the doctoral degree as the minimum requirement for full membership. The committee recommending the change argued that APA membership constituted a certification of competence to much of the public. By limiting itself to doctoral recipients the association could not only protect prospective clients but also lessen competition in the increasingly lucrative field of private practice. In the seventies psychologists sought the recognition of major health insurance companies (especially Blue Cross/Blue Shield), and they believed that master's-level practitioners hurt their chances of achieving parity with psychiatrists. Meanwhile they looked ahead to winning their share of the ultimate jackpot—a federally sponsored program for national health insurance.

The APA clearly did not represent psychologists who held only master's degrees. About 75 percent of association members had doctorates, while at most 20 percent of master's level practitioners belonged to the APA. When the association went to court to deny the designation "qualified mental health professional" to any psychologist without a doctorate, it dealt a deliberate blow to the interests of its less educated minority. Nor was the dispute confined to the clinical field. The APA's California affiliate, for example, failed to support a certification bill for school psychologists; the latter then responded by forming an independent group to secure the legislation. In other parts of the country school psychologists, few of whom held doctorates, came to doubt that the APA could serve their interests on the national level. In 1969 they formed the National Association of School Psychologists, which they hoped would effectively represent the practitioners in their field. In the mid-seventies some master's-level clinicians wondered if they too needed a separate organization.

The wartime dreams of unity crumbled under the weight of psychology's conflicting interests. No matter how hard they tried, the leaders of the APA could not provide each group of psychologists with everything it wanted. As planned during the war, new divisions arose to serve new interests, but the central direction of the APA continued to point toward increasing professionalism, primarily in the clinical field. Groups with other goals formed their own organizations. In 1959 academic purists established the Psychonomic Society, which closely resembled the APA of the thirties in size, aims, and decorum. Three years later the "humanists," who believed professional qualifications were becoming overly formalistic, set up the American Association for Humanistic Psychology. Soon thereafter came the American Psychologists for Social Action, the Association for Women Psychologists, and the Association of Black Psychologists. Other new groups emerged to speak for other interests. In 1971 even some clinical psychologists found the need to act. Believing that the APA was not pursuing professional goals with sufficient diligence, they formed the Council for the Advancement of Psychological Professions and Sciences to lobby for legal equality with psychiatrists.

For the most part, psychologists formed splinter groups to supplement rather than replace the APA. Despite endless controversy, the association continued to grow because it still managed to provide at least something for all of its members. Occasionally the APA acted clearly in the public interest as well. The rules it helped to formulate for the development of psychological tests, for example, had a benign influence on test publishers and indirectly on test takers. Usually, however, the quest for professional status had its largest effect on the psychologists themselves. In the seventies a few practitioners urged some rethinking about the nature and desirability of professionalism, but their arguments could do little to dissuade those colleagues who saw the illusive prize coming nearer their grasp. In 1974, for instance, the APA launched the National Registry of Health Service Providers in Psychology, an ambitious new certification scheme designed to convince the government and insurance companies that psychologists could equal the qualifications of psychiatrists. Thus the quest for professionalism did not falter, and the leaders of the APA continued to believe that the final goal was both beneficial and attainable.

Applied psychologists emerged from the Second World War well prepared to move further down the road to professionalism. Unlike their counterparts at the end of World War 1, they had over six years of military experience in which to refine their techniques. More important perhaps, they had for the first time an effective national organization working in their behalf. The breach between research and application seemed to have closed, and practitioners were in a position to act on professional issues without first having to overcome the resistance of their academic colleagues. Applied psychologists were ready to meet the postwar demand for their services and to channel it for their own purposes. They did not anticipate the size and nature of that demand, however, and they were thus pushed in directions not entirely of their own choosing.

The Veterans Administration's vast program to train and employ clinical psychologists helped to stamp the marks of professionalism on clinicians much more quickly and completely than on practitioners in other applied fields. Widespread popular interest supplemented the needs of the federal government, and private practice became an attractive, if still not entirely legitimate, alternative to work in hospitals and psychiatric clinics. Thus the professional problems of clinical psychology, which essentially involved struggles with psychiatrists, came to absorb almost all the attention of the APA and the state organizations. The interests of school and industrial psychologists got lost in the drive to turn clinical psychology into a full-fledged "health profession." Graduate training for nonclinicians drifted away from psychology departments and into schools of education and business. The graduates of these programs were less likely to feel at home in the APA than in one of the divisions of the American Personnel and Guidance Association or in similar groups. Psychologists succeeded quite well in regulating practitioners in the clinical field, but they failed to impose their standards of professionalism on the many workers who offered other kinds of psychological service.

Applied psychology also began to fragment over the desirability of its fundamental service—human adjustment. Many clinicians came to see themselves as "health service providers" whose job was to treat mental illness and whose skill equaled that of the psychiatrist. In their rush to become ersatz physicians, these clinical psychologists abandoned the claim that they performed a service unique to psychology. Meanwhile other practitioners broadened the notion of adjustment to include modifying the environment as well as the individual. In the sixties all the applied fields took a strong dose of social psychology and came forth with a new interest in organizations and communities. But in trying to operate on this level applied psychologists were clearly reaching beyond the realm of their exclusive competence. Practitioners of all kinds were thus feeling increasingly constrained by the idea and practice of adjustment. No one knew, however, if they could find a suitable replacement and still claim professional status.

One thing appeared certain: the demand for applied psychologists would continue to expand. The growing complexity of society put more Americans in need of adjustment than ever before. To an increasing extent, large-scale organizations—businesses, schools, government agencies —required that each person be fitted into his proper niche. Meanwhile individuals found themselves increasingly unable to cope with the fragmentation and isolation that modern society produced. The applied psychologists could claim to attack both problems at once. Indeed, they could argue that the well-adjusted society—however gray and lifeless it might appear to some—remained the only utopian dream that could ever be realized in the United States. Events of the postwar era, however, gave little indication that applied psychologists had any coherent vision of the role they might one day play in American society. They seemed to pursue professional status without much understanding of what they would do if they got it. Psychology's great postwar prosperity appeared to blind practitioners to the desirability of either a close relationship with academicians or a sense of unity among themselves. Thus, the demand for applied psychologists would expand, but it would probably be met not by a single profession but by a jumble of conflicting groups.

CONCLUSION

In April 1972 the *APA Monitor* ran a cartoon that showed two psychologists chatting in front of a television set. The program was changing from "Marcus Welby, M.D." to "Owen Marshall, Counselor-at-Law." "You say you *know* when psychology will have 'made it'?" asked one. "Yes," his companion replied. "When there is a Nobel Prize for psychology?" suggested the first. "No," his colleague responded. "When we are included in national health insurance?" "No." "When?" "When we have our own TV hero!"[1] A few months later psychologists got a television hero of sorts. He did not appear as a sturdy public servant in an hour-long melodrama, however; TV's psychologist turned out to be a pleasant but insecure psychotherapist in a half-hour situation comedy. Although "The Bob Newhart Show" provided some sign of the public acceptance of psychologists, it also indicated that psychology was not to be taken quite as seriously as medicine or law. Psychologists had their television hero, but their quest for professional status would have to continue.

A clearer indication of how successfully psychology had "made it" as a profession came in the surveys of occupational prestige. The first extensive postwar poll put psychologists high on the list—ahead of schoolteachers, social workers, and civil engineers and only one step below priests, lawyers, and architects.[2] It was a creditable showing, especially for an occupation that had barely existed thirty years before. Still, the psychologists had room for further progress: 15 percent of those surveyed did not know what ranking to give psychologists, and those groups with which psychologists preferred to identify themselves—physicians, scientists, and college professors—rated well above them in the poll. While it is largely futile to try to determine if and when psychology "really" became a profession, the surveys indicated that by the end of World War 2 psychologists had as much public prestige as many occupations that were generally considered professional.

The psychologists' progress on the road to professionalism can be explained in part by events that psychologists themselves controlled. The most important struggle was for an organization that would concern itself with professional issues. The years after World War 1 saw repeated efforts to establish such a group: the Clinical Section of the American Psychological Association was formed in 1919, the Association of Consulting Psychologists in 1930, and the American Association for Applied Psychology in 1937. Although each of these organizations successively assumed more control over psychological practice, it was the slow involvement of the American Psychological Association in professional matters that gave practitioners their first genuinely effective agency for the professionalization of psychology. Only when the APA became concerned with the widening of psychological practice and with the subsidiary issues of certification, ethical behavior, and standardized training could applied psychologists move to acquire the attributes of recognized professions.

The applied psychologists faced an unusually wide range of opposition to their quest for professional status. Like other occupational groups on the road to professionalism, they encountered practitioners who lacked any formal training in the field and whom they consequently decried as charlatans. Such people posed a constant threat to the reputation of genuine psychologists, but neither public exposés nor state certification proved effective in driving them out of business. Because the results of inept or fraudulent practice were much more difficult to uncover in psychology than in medicine or engineering, the elimination of some of the competition from charlatans awaited advances in psychological techniques.

In addition, applied psychology, unlike occupations that began professionalizing in the nineteenth century, met resistance from groups that were already well professionalized. One was the prestigious medical profession, which lent support to its most poorly established practitioners, the psychiatrists, in their attempts to restrain the rise of applied psychology. The other source of opposition was psychology's academic community, which was reluctant to use its domination of the APA and control of psychological training to promote applied work. While applied psychologists might have expected to displace the amateurs and the frauds, they realized that they had no chance to vanquish such well-established groups as physicians and college professors. The quest for professional status thus involved not only overcoming the charlatans but also reaching a modus vivendi with occupations that were already highly professionalized.

The progress that applied psychologists made toward professional status cannot be attributed solely to their own efforts. The rapid social changes of the twentieth century, especially the growth of impersonal, large-scale organizations, left the American public—individuals and administrators—in need of assistance in adjustment. By promising to apply the principles and techniques of science to adjustment problems, applied psychologists moved to meet a large and growing demand for psychological services. Psychologists saw themselves traveling with the tides of history, and they realized that they were not merely fabricating requests for their services out of a desire to attain professional status. Although modernization in a sense produced the demand for applied psychology, practitioners did not benefit from every advance in the modernizing process. In the thirties, for example, psychological practice grew less rapidly than the expansion of services by the federal government. Thus, no matter how much applied psychologists were able to do for themselves, the varying public demand for psychological services provided a crucial element in the professionalization of psychology.

The most critical example of the interplay of internal and external forces in applied psychology's quest for professional status came during World War 2. The war witnessed the greatest mobilization of resources in American history. The urgency of the struggle made it more necessary than ever before that each person—especially those in the armed forces—be placed in his most productive job and kept at work until peace returned. The problem, which was essentially one of adjustment, produced an unprecedented demand for psychological services. At the same time psychologists saw an unparalleled opportunity to expand their activities. Psychological organizations made early contacts with the military, and they later established an effective placement agency to maximize the contribution of psychologists to the war effort. Even the reorganization of the APA, which might appear to be a purely internal operation, took place in part to allow psychologists to respond with a single voice to the greatly expanded demand for psychological services which the war had initiated. Observers may differ in their assessment of the relative importance of the military's needs for a well-adjusted work force and the psychologists' efforts to professionalize themselves. But no one can doubt that applied psychology entered the war weak, splintered, and devoid of much public confidence; and emerged from it unified, strengthened, and invigorated by an unprecedented popular demand.

Nothing like the Second World War is likely to happen again. Other academic specialists currently hoping to gain professional status cannot count on a social cataclysm to help them along, and they may have trouble arguing that modern society has some essential need for their services. So while the sociologists, geographers, historians, and the like will face most of the problems encountered by applied psychology, they must proceed without some of its most important advantages. They are, however, at least in a position to ask themselves whether professional status is worth the struggle needed to attain it.

BIBLIOGRAPHICAL NOTE

MANUSCRIPT COLLECTIONS

The papers of the American Psychological Association, located in the Library of Congress, provide an extremely important source for organizational developments within psychology, especially for the regimes of Secretaries Donald G. Paterson (1931-1937) and Willard C. Olson (1937-1945). The collection includes not only the papers of the APA itself but also those of the American Association for Applied Psychology. The collection in the archives of the History of American Psychology at the University of Akron is of less value on organizational issues. The Margaret Ives Papers, which are located there, do contain much information on the founding of the National Council of Women Psychologists, however. I have also cited documents from the Willard C. Olson, Dorothea McCarthy, and Boder Museum Papers, all of which are also available in the archives. There is no convenient manuscript collection for the Psychologists League, but I was able to examine some documents furnished me by a former league president, Daniel Harris of San Diego, California.

GENERAL WORKS

No general history of applied psychology exists. The standard intellectual history of the discipline is Edwin G. Boring, *A History of Experimental Psychology,* 2nd ed. (New York: Appleton-Century-Crofts, 1950). It may be profitably supplemented by A. A. Roback, *History of American Psychology* (New York: Library Publishers, 1952). Personal reminiscences of the careers of early psychologists are contained in the essays in *A History of Psychology in Autobiography,* ed. by Carl Murchison, Edwin G. Boring, et al., vols. 1-4 (Worcester, Mass.: Clark University Press, 1930-1952), vol. 5 (New York: Appleton-Century-Crofts, 1967), vol. 6 (Englewood Cliffs, N.J.: Prentice-Hall, 1974).

Clinical psychology has received an informative full-length treatment in John M. Reisman, *The Development of Clinical Psychology* (New York: Appleton-Century-Crofts, 1966). A historian, Loren Baritz, has traced the use of psychologists and other social scientists in American industry in his study *The Servants of Power* (Middletown, Conn.: Wesleyan University Press, 1960). There is no detailed historical account of the work of educational psychologists. Florence L. Goodenough discusses the development of tests for school, clinic, and business in *Mental Testing: Its History, Principles, and Applications* (New York: Rinehart and Co., 1949), pp. 3-94. A useful history of mental illness which puts American psychiatrists in historical context is Albert Deutsch, *The Mentally Ill in America,* 2nd ed. (New York: Columbia University Press, 1949).

INTRODUCTION

The sociological literature on professions is extensive and growing rapidly. Elliott A. Krause provides an informative survey of the various approaches to the subject in *The Sociology of Occupations* (Boston: Little, Brown, 1971), pp. 13-105. Several anthologies of articles have recently appeared, including *Professionalization,* ed. by Howard M. Vollmer and Donald L. Mills (Englewood Cliffs, N.J.: Prentice-Hall, 1966), and *The Professions and Their Prospects,* ed. by Eliot Freidson (Beverly Hills, Cal.: Sage Publications, 1973). Freidson has also furnished an enlightening full-length analysis of physicians in *Profession of Medicine* (New York: Dodd, Mead, 1970). Sociologists have written little about psychologists, although Everett Cherrington Hughes does offer a brief analysis in "Psychology: Science and/or Profession," *American Psychologist* 7 (August 1952): 441-43.

1. THE BEGINNINGS OF APPLIED PSYCHOLOGY

An extremely useful work by a historian is Thomas M. Camfield, "Psychologists at War: The History of American Psychology and the First World War" (Ph.D. dissertation, University of Texas, 1969). Camfield discusses scientific and professional issues from 1870 to 1930 as well as events of the war. He has distilled the first two chapters into "The Professionalization of American Psychology, 1870-1917," *Journal of the History of the Behavioral Sciences* 9 (January 1973): 66-75. Samuel W. Fernberger covers developments within the APA in "The American Psychological Association: A Historical Summary, 1892-1930," *Psychological Bulletin* 29 (January 1932): 1-8.

On clinical psychology, Murray Levine and Adeline Levine devote a chapter to Lightner Witmer's clinic in *A Social History of the Helping Services* (New York: Appleton-Century-Crofts, 1970). Another useful source is John M. O'Donnell, "The Clinical Psychology of Lightner Witmer: A Case Study of Institutional Change," *Journal of the History of the Behavioral Sciences* 15 (January 1979): 3-17. An informative contemporary account of psychological clinics is Theodate L. Smith, "The Development of Psychological Clinics in the United States," *Pedagogical Seminary* 21 (March 1914): 143-53. A broad perspective on the rise of industrial psychology can be found in Morris S. Viteles, *Industrial Psychology* (New York: W. W. Norton and Co., 1932), pp. 8-56. Leonard W. Ferguson offers detailed coverage of some events in separately published chapters of *The Heritage of Industrial Psychology* (n.p.: 1962-65).

The early years of intelligence testing have received much recent attention. Thomas P. Weinland provides a full-length survey in "A History of the I.Q. in America, 1890-1940" (Ph.D. dissertation, Columbia University, 1970). Daniel J. Kevles emphasizes the army's displeasure with its testing program in "Testing the Army's Intelligence: Psychologists and the Military in World War 2," *Journal of American History* 55 (December 1968): 565-81. Joel Spring, in "Psychologists and the War: The Meaning of Intelligence in the Alpha and Beta Tests," *History of Education Quarterly* 12 (spring 1972): 3-15, argues that the tests measured only the ability to function in complex organizations. Psychologists have been debating the effects of intelligence testing. Leon J. Kamin in "The Science and Politics of I.Q.," *Social Research* 41 (autumn 1974): 387-425, finds that the intelligence test was a tool of oppression from its very beginnings. Franz Samelson refutes Kamin in "On the Science and Politics of the IQ," *Social Research* 42 (autumn 1975): 467-88, arguing essentially that Kamin fails to deal with the early testers in their own terms. Kamin briefly replies, ibid., 488-92. Lee J. Cronbach surveys the debate, past and present, in "Five Decades of Public Controversy over Mental Testing," *American Psychologist* 30 (January 1975): 1-14, and appends a useful bibliography.

2. ADJUSTMENT: SCIENCE, SERVICE, AND IDEAL

Adjustment has received only a smattering of attention as an aspect of social thought. The term "adjustment" is also used in Freudian theory, and it is the psychoanalytic version of the concept of adjustment that Paul Halmos examines in *The Faith of the Counsellors* (New York: Schocken Books, 1966). No discussion exists of the relationship of adjustment and professionalization.

3. THE PERILS OF POPULARITY

Grace Adams provides a critical survey of psychology in the twenties in "The Rise and Fall of Psychology," *Atlantic Monthly*, January 1934, pp. 82-92. Stephen Leacock's witty discussion, "A Manual of the New Mentality," *Harper's*, March 1924, pp. 471-80, must be read in its entirety to be fully appreciated. A good idea of the nature of American psychology and the range of psychological activities can be obtained from the American Psychological Association *Year Books*.

There are two first-rate recent analyses of Freudianism in America, but unfortunately neither deals with the postwar period. John Chynoweth Burnham, *Psychoanalysis and American Medicine 1894-1918* (New York: International Universities Press, 1967) is strictly an intellectual history, while Nathan G. Hale, Jr., *Freud and the Americans* (New York: Oxford University Press, 1971), covers the entire social scene. Behaviorism has not received comparable attention. Lucille Burnham, "Behaviorism in the 1920s," *American Quarterly* 7 (spring 1955): 15-30, is brief but interesting. She explores the connection of behaviorism to other intellectual movements in her doctoral dissertation "Behaviorism, John B. Watson, and American Social Thought" (Ph.D. dissertation, University of California, Berkeley, 1964).

Several of the works mentioned earlier are also helpful on the period between war and depression: Baritz, *The Servants of Power*, on industrial psychology; Weinland, "A History of the I.Q. in America," on educational psychology; and Reisman, *The Development of Clinical Psychology*, on clinical work. Relations between clinical psychology and psychiatry are discussed in Thomas Vernor Moore, "A Century of Psychology in Its Relationship to American Psychiatry," in *One Hundred Years of American Psychiatry*, ed. by J. K. Hall (New York: Columbia University Press, 1944) pp. 443-77, and in J. E. Wallace Wallin's autobiography, *Odyssey of a Psychologist* (Wilmington, Del.: by the author, 1955). David Shakow sharply criticizes Moore's approach and conclusions in " 'One Hundred Years of American Psychiatry': A Special Review," *Psychological Bulletin*

42 (July 1945): 423-32. In an important but unpublished supplement veteran clinical psychologists tell of their experiences with psychiatrists in responses to my 1978 questionnaire.

Events within the APA are summarized in the proceedings of its meetings, published annually in the *Psychological Bulletin.* Fernberger's "The American Psychological Association," mentioned earlier, offers useful information by an APA official. Supplementing published sources are the Clinical Section minutes (box F9) and the certification committee files (boxes D8 and D9) in the American Psychological Association Collection at the Library of Congress.

4. PSYCHOLOGISTS AND THE DEPRESSION

Lorenz J. Finison analyzes the responses of psychologists to the job crisis of the thirties in "Unemployment, Politics, and the History of Organized Psychology," *American Psychologist* 31 (November 1976): 747-55. Johnnie P. Symonds discusses the efforts of applied psychologists to establish a national organization in "Ten Years of Journalism in Psychology, 1937-1946: the First Decade of the Journal of Consulting Psychology," *Journal of Consulting Psychology* 10 (November-December 1946): 335-74. Otherwise, the best sources for professional developments in the thirties are the periodicals published by the various organizations: the *Psychological Bulletin,* the *Journal of Consulting Psychology,* the SPSSI *Bulletin,* and the *Psychologists League Journal.* Also valuable is the independently issued *Psychological Exchange,* which unfortunately ceased publication in 1936.

Among the many articles published in the thirties three are especially informative. Albert T. Poffenberger's 1935 presidential address to the APA, "Psychology and Life," *Psychological Review* 43 (January 1936): 9-31, presents the case for the association's further involvement in professional issues. S. Diamond, "The Economic Position of the Psychologist," *Psychological Exchange* 4 (October 1935): 5-8, views the professional status of psychology from a position outside the psychological establishment. Finally, Douglas Fryer, "Applied and Professional Attitudes," *Journal of Consulting Psychology* 3 (January-February 1939): 1-10 outlines the goals of the AAAP.

Published sources fail to illuminate many of the organizational issues that arose in the thirties. The APA Collection at the Library of Congress, including as it does the papers of the AAAP as well as the older association, fills several important gaps.

The state of applied psychology before the war is shown in the text by J. Stanley Gray, *Psychology in Use* (New York: American Book Co., 1941).

5. PSYCHOLOGISTS AND THE WAR

There is no satisfactory account of applied psychology in World War 2. Psychologists made plans to produce a general history of their role in the war but never carried them through. One brief discussion exists–Eugénie Chmielniski, "Influence de la guerre sur les applications de la psychologie aux U.S.A.," *Enfance* 1 (1948): 176-84–but the detailed story appears only in pieces scattered through many sources.

Walter R. Miles discusses the early mobilization of psychologists in "Preparations of Psychology for the War," n.d. (typewritten), APA collection, box G8. His presentation is supplemented by Horace B. English's correspondence on the subject in the APA Collection, box K10.

A general account of psychology in the army during the war appears in U.S., Department of the Army, Office, Chief of Research and Development, *The Research Psychologist in the Army, 1917 to 1967*, by J. E. Uhlaner, Technical Research Report 1155 (Washington: U.S. Army Behavioral Science Research Laboratory, 1968), pp. 10-19. Walter V. Bingham with James Rorty discusses psychological contributions to army personnel work in "How the Army Sorts Its Man Power," *Harper's*, September 1942, pp. 432-40. More detail may be found in the articles written by the Personnel Research Section in wartime issues of the *Psychological Bulletin*.

Morris S. Viteles recounts the work of the Committee on Selection and Training of Aircraft Pilots in "The Aircraft Pilot: Five Years of Research: A Summary of Outcomes," *Psychological Bulletin* 42 (October 1945): 489-526. The air force's program is summarized in Arthur R. Kooker, "Basic Military Training and Classification of Personnel," in *The Army Air Forces in World War 2*, vol. 6, *Men and Planes*, ed. by Wesley Frank Craven and James Lea Cate (Chicago: University of Chicago Press, 1955), pp. 537-56. John C. Flanagan provides more detail in *The Aviation Psychology Program in the Army Air Forces*, Army Air Forces Aviation Psychology Program Research Report No. 1 (Washington: Government Printing Office, 1948), which is but the first of nineteen volumes on the subject.

A discussion of personnel work in the navy may be found in Dewey B. Stuit, ed., *Personnel Research and Test Development in the Bureau of Naval Personnel* (Princeton, N.J.: Princeton University Press, 1947). Charles W. Bray explains the work of the Applied Psychology Panel in *Psychology and Military Proficiency* (Princeton, N.J.: Princeton University Press 1948).

Morton A. Seidenfeld provides a valuable account of the army's clinical program in "Clinical Psychology," *Neuropsychiatry in World War 2*, vol. 1, *Zone of Interior*, ed. by Albert J. Glass and Robert J. Bernucci (Washington: Office of the Surgeon General, Department of the Army, 1966), pp. 567-603. Psychiatry's role in the war receives thorough treatment in William C. Menninger, *Psychiatry in a Troubled World: Yesterday's War and Today's Challenge* (New York: Macmillan, 1948).

Dorwin Cartwright surveys the work of social psychologists in "Social Psychology in the United States during the Second World War," *Human Relations* 1, no. 3 (1948): 333-52. A picture of psychologists' utilization by the military emerges from the data presented by Steuart Henderson Britt and Jane D. Morgan in "Military Psychologists in World War 2," *American Psychologist* 1 (October 1946): 423-37.

Finally, many informative articles appeared during the war in the *Psychological Bulletin*, which had a regular section on "Psychology and the War," and in the *Journal of Consulting Psychology*.

6. PREPARATIONS FOR PROSPERITY

Johnnie P. Symonds summarizes some of the organizational developments in "Ten Years of Journalism in Psychology," mentioned earlier. For further information on the AAAP readers should consult the "Summarized Proceedings and Reports" in the *Journal of Consulting Psychology*. The journal also printed many articles on professional issues which give a good indication of the problems perceived by practitioners. The best sources for events within the APA are the proceedings of the annual meetings, which were compiled by Willard C. Olson and published in the *Psychological Bulletin*. Samuel Fernberger points out the growing professionalism of the APA in his short historical account "The American Psychological Association, 1892-1942," *Psychological Review* 50 (January 1943): 33-60.

Karl Dallenbach has written a thorough report, "The Emergency Committee in Psychology, National Research Council," *American Journal of Psychology* 59 (October 1946): 496-582, which provides important information on the emergency committee. The first director of the OPP discusses the beginnings of that agency in Steuart Henderson Britt, "The Office of Psychological Personnel: Report of the First Six Months," *Psychological Bulletin* 39 (November 1942): 773-93.

A series of reports outlines developments in the reorganization of the APA. Yerkes's subcommittee presents its findings and recommendations in Edwin G. Boring et al., "First Report of the Subcommittee on Survey and Planning for Psychology," *Psychological Bulletin* 39 (October 1942): 619-30, and "Psychology as Science and Profession," ibid. (November 1942), 761-72. A copy of the Condensed Transcript of the Intersociety Convention, 29-31 May 1943, is available in the APA Collection, box 16. "Recommendations of the Intersociety Constitutional Convention of Psychologists," *Psychological Bulletin* 40 (November 1943): 621-47, includes the first published version of the new bylaws.

Much of the debate over reorganizing the APA never reached print. Correspondence in the APA Collection, box K4, contains sharper disagreements than appear, for example, in "The Proposed AAAP-APA Merger," *Journal of Consulting Psychology* 8 (March-April 1944): 118-24, and the promerger rebuttal, Albert T. Poffenberger and Alice I. Bryan, "Toward Unification in Psychology," ibid. (July-August 1944): 253-57.

7. APPLIED PSYCHOLOGY IN THE POSTWAR ERA

Although there are no general treatments of applied psychology in the postwar era, psychologists did produce a series of books that, taken together, outline professional developments in the period. The interested reader may consult: Robert S. Daniel and C. M. Louttit, *Professional Problems in Psychology* (New York: Prentice-Hall, 1953); Robert I. Watson, *Psychology As a Profession* (Garden City, N.Y.: Doubleday and Co., 1954); Kenneth E. Clark, *America's Psychologists* (Washington: American Psychological Association, 1957); Wilse B. Webb, ed., *The Profession of Psychology* (New York: Holt, Rinehart and Winston, 1962); Kenneth E. Clark and George A. Miller, eds., *Psychology* (Englewood Cliffs, N.J.: Prentice-Hall, 1970); and Benjamin M. Braginsky and Dorothea D. Braginsky, *Mainstream Psychology: A Critique* (New York: Holt, Rinehart and Winston, 1974). In addition, William Goode surveys the first half of the period from a sociologist's perspective in "Encroachment, Charlatanism, and the Emerging Profession: Psychology, Medicine, and Sociology," *American Sociological Review* 25 (December 1960): 902-14.

Two books are of special interest on specific applied fields. William A. Hunt analyzes the clinician's role in *The Clinical Psychologist* (Springfield, Ill.: Charles C. Thomas, 1956), and Susan W. Gray discusses school psychology in *The Psychologist in the Schools* (New York: Holt, Rinehart and Winston, 1963). Nothing comparable exists for industrial psychology, although there are informative texts available in that field and the others as well.

The periodical literature on the many aspects of professional psychology is vast and probably beyond mastery. Fortunately, *The American Psychologist* (1946-) provides an excellent source for developments within the applied fields and the APA. The association has recently inaugurated two new periodicals, *Professional Psychology* (1969-) and the *APA Monitor* (1970-), both of which contain many helpful articles. The various applied fields and interest groups have their journals as well, with the result that at least two sides of every issue are available somewhere in print.

NOTES

INTRODUCTION

1. Datamate advertisement, *San Francisco Sunday Examiner and Chronicle,* 26 May 1974, Datebook sec., p. 26.
2. "Coming On Strong," *Newsweek,* 13 October 1975, p. 64; *Sacramento Bee,* 10 July 1975, p. A16; Nancy Henderson, "Writer's Block: 1. Three Successful Cases of Writer's Block Therapy," *Writer's Digest,* August 1975, pp. 16-17.
3. Eileen Milling, "A New Way to Improve Effectiveness on the Job," *Nation's Business,* July 1975, p. 65; J. R. Block, "Attention Failure: A Test That Tells Who Is Accident-Prone," *Psychology Today,* June 1975, pp. 84-85.
4. A. M. Carr-Saunders, "Professionalization in Historical Perspective," in *Professionalization,* ed. Howard M. Vollmer and Donald L. Mills (Englewood Cliffs, N. J.: Prentice-Hall, 1966), p. 4; Ernest Greenwood, "The Elements of Professionalization," ibid., pp. 10-18.
5. Julius A. Roth, "Professionalism: The Sociologist's Decoy," *Sociology of Work and Occupations* 1 (January 1974): 18.
6. Oscar Handlin, foreword, in Daniel H. Calhoun, *Professional Lives in America* (Cambridge, Mass.: Harvard University Press, 1965), pp. vii-viii.

1. THE BEGINNINGS OF APPLIED PSYCHOLOGY

1. A. A. Roback, *History of American Psychology* (New York: Library Publishers, 1952), p. 174.
2. Frederick Jackson Turner, "The Significance of the Frontier in American History," in *The Frontier in American History* (New York: Holt, Rinehart and Winston, 1962), p. 38.
3. Turner, "Social Forces in American History," ibid., pp. 312-19.
4. Samuel W. Fernberger, "The American Psychological Association: A Historical Summary," *Psychological Bulletin* 29 (January 1932): 22.
5. Murray Levine and Adeline Levine, *A Social History of Helping Services* (New York: Appleton-Century-Corfts, 1970), p. 56.
6. Leonard W. Ferguson, "Walter Dill Scott," in *The Heritage of Industrial Psychology* (n. p.: the author? 1962-65), p. 1.
7. Loren Baritz, *The Servants of Power* (Middletown, Conn.: Wesleyan University Press, 1960), p. 36.

8. Henry H. Goddard, *The Kallikak Family* (New York: Macmillan, 1912), p. 104.

9. Fernberger, p. 46.

10. Thomas M. Camfield, "Psychologists at War: The History of American Psychology and the First World War" (Ph.D. diss. University of Texas, 1969), p. 87.

11. James R. Angell quoted ibid., p. 127.

12. Henry P. McCain quoted in Ferguson, "Psychology and the Army," p. 144.

13. Camfield, p. 144.

14. Ibid.

15. Daniel J. Kevles, "Testing the Army's Intelligence: Psychologists and the Military in World War 1," *Journal of American History* 55 (December 1968): 578-81.

16. I am grateful to Kerry W. Buckley for the information on the Economic Psychology Association.

2. ADJUSTMENT: Science, Service, and Ideal

1. A. T. Poffenberger, *Applied Psychology: Its Principles and Methods* (New York: D. Appleton, 1927), p. 6.

2. Gertrude H. Hildreth, *Psychological Service for School Problems* (Yonkers-on-Hudson, N. Y.: World Book Co., 1930), p. 1.

3. Harold Ernest Burtt, *Psychology of Advertising* (Boston: Houghton Mifflin, 1938), pp. 3, 461.

4. Laurence Frederic Shaffer, *The Psychology of Adjustment: An Objective Approach to Mental Hygiene* (Boston: Houghton Mifflin, 1936), p. 3.

5. Lawrence Augustus Averill, *The Hygiene of Instruction* (Boston: Houghton Mifflin, 1928), preface [n.p.].

6. John E. Anderson and Florence L. Goodenough, *Your Child, Year by Year,* 4th ed. (New York: Parents' Magazine, 1934), p. ix.

7. Francis F. Powers et al., *Psychology in Everyday Living* (Boston: D. C. Heath, 1938), p. 252.

8. Richard Wellington Husband, *Applied Psychology* (New York: Harper, 1934), p. 1.

9. Averill, p. 14.

10. Harry Walker Hepner, *Finding Yourself in Your Work* (New York: D. Appleton-Century, 1937), p. 137.

11. Morris S. Viteles, *Industrial Psychology* (New York: Norton, 1932), p. 4.

12. Douglas Fryer, *Vocational Self Guidance* (Philadelphia: Lippincott, 1925), pp. 11-20.

13. Sadie Myers Shellow, *How to Develop Your Personality* (New York: Harper, 1932), p. 27.

14. Morris S. Viteles, *The Science of Work* (New York: Norton, 1934), p. 41.

15. Percival M. Symonds, *Psychological Diagnosis in Social Adjustment* (New York: American Book Co., 1934), pp. 83-84.

16. Harry Walker Hepner, *Human Relations in Changing Industry* (New York: Prentice-Hall, 1934), p. 14.

17. Hepner, *Finding Yourself in Your Work,* pp. 44-45.

18. Floyd L. Ruch, *Psychology and Life* (Chicago: Scott, Foresman, 1937) p. 45.

19. J. E. Wallace Wallin, *Personality Maladjustments and Mental Hygiene* (New York: McGraw-Hill, 1935), p. 45.

3. THE PERILS OF POPULARITY

1. Stephen Leacock, "A Manual of the New Mentality," *Harper's* 148 (March 1924): 472-73.

2. William E. Leuchtenburg, *The Perils of Prosperity, 1914-1932* (Chicago: University of Chicago Press, 1958), p. 164. See also Grace Adams, "The Rise and Fall of Psychology," *Atlantic Monthly,* January 1934, pp. 82-90.

3. John B. Watson, *Behaviorism* (New York: People's Institute Publishing Co., 1924), p. 238.

4. Donald G. Paterson, "A Note on Popular Pseudo-Psychological Beliefs," *Journal of Applied Psychology* 7 (March 1923): 101.

5. Dorothy Yates, *Psychological Racketeers* (Boston: Richard G. Badger, 1932), p. 199. Italics in original.

6. Morris S. Viteles, "The Clinical Viewpoint in Vocational Selection," *Journal of Applied Psychology* 9 (1925): 131-38. Quotation is from p. 134.

7. James McKeen Cattell, "The Psychological Corporation," *Annals* 110 (November 1923): 166.

8. Thomas Pogue Weinland, "A History of the I.Q. in America, 1890-1941" (Ph.D. diss., Columbia University, 1970), pp. 183-210.

9. Ernest W. Tiegs, "The Faith of Our Fathers," *American School Board Journal* 83 (July 1931): 46, quoted ibid., p. 246.

10. J. E. Wallace Wallin, *Odyssey of a Psychologist*, (Wilmington, Del.: by the author, 1955), p. 83.

11. R. S. Woodworth quoted in Carl E. Seashore, *Pioneering in Psychology* (Iowa City: University of Iowa Press, 1942), p. 131.

12. Wallin, pp. 69-84.

13. Poll of clinical psychologists taken by the author in letters of 9 March 1978. All psychologists who belonged to the AAAP Clinical Section in 1941 and whose addresses appeared in the 1976 *APA Yearbook* were sent the questionnaire. A total of 138 were sent the questionnaire and 75 responded.

14. "The Relation between Psychiatry and Psychology (A Symposium)," *Psychological Exchange* 2 (October-November 1933): 153.

15. Andrew W. Brown, "The Meeting of the Clinical Section of the American Psychological Association," *Psychological Exchange* 2 (October-November 1933) 176. The quotation is from Brown, who was reporting on Morgan's remarks.

16. Ibid., p. 177.

17. Wallin, p. 84.

18. J. E. Wallace Wallin, "Shall We Continue to Train Clinical Psychologists for Second-String Jobs?" *Psychological Clinic* 18 (January 1930): 242-45.

19. Certificate of Frederic Lyman Wells, 10 September 1923, American Psychological Association Collection, Library of Congress, Washington, D.C. (hereinafter, APA Coll.), box I11.

20. Fernberger, p. 49.

21. Confidential memorandum to the council, [December? 1926], APA Coll., box D9; Frederic Lyman Wells to Samuel W. Fernberger, 4 December 1926, APA Coll., box D9.

22. Margaret Floy Washburn to Frederic Lyman Wells, 15 September 1927, APA Coll., box D9.

23. Samuel W. Fernberger, "The American Psychological Association: A Historical Summary," *Psychological Bulletin* 29 (January 1932): p. 53.

4. PSYCHOLOGISTS AND THE DEPRESSION

1. "Page the Psychologists," editorial, *New York Times*, 1 January 1934, p. 22.

2. Grace Adams, "The Rise and Fall of Psychology," *Atlantic Monthly*, January 1934, p. 90.

3. Harold E. Burtt, review of *Faith, Fear and Fortunes* by Daniel Starch, in *Journal of Applied Psychology* 18 (1934): 725.

4. Walter V. Bingham, "The Future of Industrial Psychology," *Journal of Consulting Psychology* 1 (January-February 1937): 10.

5. Editorial, *Psychological Exchange* 1 (August 1932): 3; J. E. W. Wallin, letter to the editor in "Readers' Forum," *Psychological Exchange* 2 (October-November 1933): 199-200; "A Tentative Formulation of a W.P.A. Project to Provide for a National Consultation Bureau," [August? 1936], APA Coll., box I11.

6.   Percival M. Symonds, "Every School Should Have a Psychologist," *School and Society,* 9 September 1933, pp. 321-29; "Meetings," *Psychological Exchange* 2 (June-July 1933): 67-68; Rose G. Anderson, "Concerning School Psychologists," *Psychological Clinic* 21 (March-May 1933): 44-46.

7.   Albert T. Poffenberger, "Psychology and Life," *Psychological Review* 43 (January 1936): 9-31.

8.   Donald G. Paterson, *Proceedings of the Forty-second Annual Meeting of the American Psychological Association,* in *Psychological Bulletin* 31 (November 1934): 654, 663-64.

9.   Donald G. Paterson to Austin B. Wood, 15 January 1934, APA Coll., box I9.

10.   Donald G. Paterson to Ross Stagner, 3 June 1935, APA Coll., box D28.

11.   Albert T. Poffenberger to Donald G. Paterson, 28 October 1935, APA Coll., box D28.

12.   Leonard Carmichael to Donald G. Paterson, 23 May 1935, APA Coll., box H8.

13.   Donald G. Paterson to I. Krechevsky, 21 April 1936; I. Krechevsky to Donald G. Paterson, 8 May 1936; Donald G. Paterson to I. Krechevsky, 12 May 1936; APA Coll., box I12.

14.   "Purpose of the S.P.S.S.I.," Society for the Psychological Study of Social Issues, *Bulletin* 1 (February 1937): 2.

15.   "Constitution of the Psychologists' League," *Psychologists' League Journal* 1 (January-February 1937): 15; ibid., (March-April 1937): 10.

16.   "League Marches," *Psychologists' League Journal* 1 (March-April 1937): 20.

17.   Poffenberger, p. 19.

18.   S. Diamond, "The Economic Position of the Psychologist," *Psychological Exchange* 4 (October 1935): 7.

19.   Horace B. English to Solomon Diamond, 27 October 1938, APA Coll., box K12; Horace B. English to C. M. Louttit, 3 April 1940, APA Coll., box K1.

20.   Association of Consulting Psychologists, "Proposed Code of Professional Ethics," *Psychological Exchange* 2 (April-May 1933): 11-12.

21.   Edward B. Greene to Donald G. Paterson, 12 November 1934 and 20 November 1934, APA Coll., box F4.

22.   Donald G. Paterson to Edward B. Greene, 14 November 1934 and 1 December 1934, APA Coll., box F4.

23.   "Conclusion of the Monthly Meetings for the Current Year," *News Letter of the Association of Consulting Psychologists* 1 (April 1935): 4-5; "New Committees," ibid., (3 June 1935), 12.

24.   Edgar A. Doll to Donald G. Paterson, 25 March 1936; Donald G. Paterson to Edgar A. Doll, 30 March 1936 and 4 May 1936, APA Coll., box H1.

25.   W.[alter] V. B.[ingham], "Salutatory," *Journal of Consulting Psychology* 2 (January-February 1938): 31. Those pictured: James McKeen Cattell, Lewis M. Terman, E. L. Thorndike, Walter Van Dyke Bingham, Leta S. Hollingworth, Robert M. Yerkes, Douglas Fryer, Robert S. Woodworth, Lightner Witmer, Henry H. Goddard, A. T. Poffenberger, and L. L. Thurstone.

26.   John E. Anderson, "Proposed Constitution of the American Association of Applied Psychologists," *Journal of Consulting Psychology* 2 (July-August 1938): 107-8.

27.   Andrew W. Brown to Milton A. Saffir, 5 January 1938, and Andrew W. Brown to H. Meltzer, 15 March 1938, APA Coll., box C1.

28.   Horace B. English to Henry Feinberg, 27 October 1938; Henry Feinberg to Horace B. English, 10 July 1939, APA Coll., box E1.

29.   Horace B. English to Gordon Allport, 17 April 1938, APA Coll., box K7.

30.   Poll of clinical psychologists, 9 March 1978.

5. PSYCHOLOGISTS AND THE WAR

1. Horace B. English to Walter R. Miles, 18 July 1940, APA Coll., box K10; Florence L. Goodenough quoted in Louise Omwake, "Psychology–in the War and After (1)," *Junior College Journal* 14 (September 1943): 20.
2. Carrol C. Pratt, introduction to "Military Psychology," *Psychological Bulletin* 38 (June 1941): 312.
3. Gordon W. Allport, "Psychological Service for Civilian Morale," *Journal of Consulting Psychology* 5 (September-October 1941): 238.
4. Horace B. English to Karl M. Dallenbach, 16 December 1938; Horace B. English to Emory S. Adams, 14 December 1938; Emory S. Adams to Horace B. English, 19 December 1938; APA Coll., box K10.
5. "U.S. Starts Program of Psychological Research," *Science News Letter,* 30 September 1939, p. 217.
6. John G. Jenkins, "Selection and Training of Aircraft Pilots," *Journal of Consulting Psychology* 5 (September-October 1941): 228-34.
7. John C. Flanagan, ed., "The Aviation Psychology Program in the Army Air Forces," Army Air Forces Aviation Psychology Program Research Report no. 1 (Washington: Government Printing Office, 1948), p. 15.
8. Frederick B. Davis, ed., "The AAF Qualifying Examination," Army Air Forces Aviation Psychology Research Report no. 6 (Washington: Government Printing Office, 1947), p. 8.
9. "Possible Psychological Contributions in a National Emergency," minutes of AAAP round table 25, 26 November 1939, pp. 11-12, APA Coll., box K10.
10. C. M. Louttit, "Psychological Work in the United States Navy," *Journal of Consulting Psychology* 5 (September-October 1941): 226-27.
11. John G. Jenkins, "Naval Aviation Psychology: (1), The Field Service Organization," *Psychological Bulletin* 42 (November 1945): 632.
12. William A. Hunt, "Clinical Psychology in the Navy," *Journal of Clinical Psychology* 1 (April 1945): 99.
13. Horace B. English, memorandum from the executive secretary, 24 May 1939, APA Coll., box K10.
14. Franklin D. Roosevelt to Henry L. Stimson, 4 December 1944, in William C. Menninger, *Psychiatry in a Troubled World* (New York: Macmillan, 1948), p. 296.
15. Morton A. Seidenfeld, "Psychological Services for the Individual in the Armed Forces," *Journal of Clinical Psychology* 1 (April 1945): 94.
16. Morton A. Seidenfeld, "Clinical Psychology," in *Neuropsychiatry in World War 2,* vol. 1, *Zone of Interior,* ed., Albert J. Glass and Robert J. Bernucci (Washington: Office of the Surgeon General, Department of the Army, 1966), p. 601.
17. Rensis Likert, "Democracy in Agriculture: Why and How?" in *Farmers in a Changing World, The Yearbook of Agriculture, 1940* (Washington: Government Printing Office, 1940), p. 999.
18. Joy P. Guilford, "Some Lessons from Aviation Psychology," *American Psychologist* 3 (January 1948): 4.
19. Walter V. Bingham, "Lessons from the Second World War," in *Progès de la psychotechnique, 1939-1945,* ed. Franziska Baumgarten (Bern, Switzerland: A. Francke, 1949), p. 139.
20. Eugénie Chmielniski, "Influence de la guerre sur les applications de la psychologie aux U.S.A.," *Enfance* 1 (1948): 184. [My translation–D.N.]
21. Charles W. Bray, *Psychology and Military Efficiency* (Princeton, N. J.: Princeton University Press, 1948), p. xi.
22. Jenkins, p. 634.
23. Walter V. Bingham with James Rorty, "How the Army Sorts Its Man Power," *Harper's,* September 1942, p. 429.
24. Lybrand Palmer Smith, foreword to *Psychology and Military Proficiency,* by Charles W. Bray (Princeton, N. J.: Princeton University Press, 1948), p. v.

25. Menninger, p. 245; Arthur R. Kooker, "Basic Military Training and Classification of Personnel," in *The Army Air Forces in World War 2,* vol. 6, *Men and Planes,* ed. Wesley Frank Craven and James Lea Cate (Chicago: University of Chicago Press, 1955), p. 556.

6. PREPARATIONS FOR PROSPERITY

1. C. M. Louttit, "Psychology during the War and Afterward," *Journal of Consulting Psychology* [hereinafter *JCP*] 8 (January-February 1944): 4.
2. Ibid., p. 7.
3. John G. Jenkins, "A Departmental Program in Psychotechnology," *JCP* 3 (March-April 1939): 54.
4. Carl R. Rogers, "Needed Emphases in the Training of Clinical Psychologists," *JCP* 3 (September-October 1939): 141-43.
5. Ibid., p. 142.
6. Milton A. Saffir, "Practical Issues in the Enactment of Legislation for Certification of Psychologists," *JCP* 5 (March-April 1941): 70-73; "Résumé of Pennsylvania Round Table on Licensing of Psychologists," ibid., 78-79.
7. Horace B. English to Elaine F. Kinder, 3 October 1939, APA Coll., box C1; C. M. Louttit to Arthur W. Kornhauser, 12 March 1941, APA Coll., box K7.
8. "American Psychological Association, 1939," *Psychologists' League Journal* 3 (September-October 1939): 87.
9. Willard C. Olson, *Proceedings of the Forty-Ninth Annual Meeting of the American Psychological Association,* in *Psychological Bulletin* 38 (November 1941): 846.
10. C. M. Louttit to Willard C. Olson, 24 April 1941, APA Coll., box E3; Horace B. English, memorandum to APA council, n.d. [8 August 1942], pp. 1-3, APA Coll., box I6.
11. Willard C. Olson, *Proceedings of the Fiftieth Annual Meeting of the American Psychological Association,* in *Psychological Bulletin* 39 (November 1942): 740.
12. Edwin G. Boring et al., "First Report of the Subcommittee on Survey and Planning for Psychology," *Psychological Bulletin* 39 (October 1942): 623-24.
13. Ibid., p. 629.
14. Karl M. Dallenbach, "The Emergency Committee in Psychology, National Research Council," *American Journal of Psychology* 59 (October 1946): 565.
15. Herbert Woodrow to Willard L. Valentine, 13 March 1943, APA Coll., box I3; Harriet O'Shea to Robert A. Brotemarkle, 2 March 1943, APA Coll., box K4.
16. John E. Anderson to Willard C. Olson, 26 May 1943, APA Coll., box I6; Carl Rogers to Alice I. Bryan, 10 May 1943, APA Coll., box K3.
17. Herman G. Canady to Ross G. Harrison, 16 March 1942, APA Coll., box H1; Steuart Henderson Britt to Herman G. Canady, 27 March 1942, APA Coll., box H1; *Proceedings of the Emergency Committee on Psychology,* 22-23 May 1942, p. 2, Willard C. Olson Papers, AHAP, box M147; Dallenbach, p. 565.
18. Gladys C. Schwesinger, "The National Council of Women Psychologists," *JCP* 7 (November-December 1943): 299.
19. Ibid., p. 301.
20. *Proceedings of the Emergency Committee in Psychology,* 22-23 October 1943, p. 41, APA Coll., box I8; italics in original; Alice I. Bryan to the author, 14 December 1977.
21. Florence L. Goodenough to Gladys Schwesinger, 29 August 1942 and 21 September 1942, Margaret Ives Papers, AHAP, box M474; Florence L. Goodenough, "Expanding Opportunities for Women Psychologists in the Post-War Period of Civil and Military Reorganization," *Psychological Bulletin* 41 (December 1944): 706-8; Florence L. Goodenough to Gladys Schwesinger, 10 June 1943 and 16 February 1943, Margaret Ives Papers, AHAP, box M474.
22. "Psychologists in Defense of Democracy," editorial, *Psychologists' League Journal* 4 (February 1941): 46.

23. Condensed transcript of the Intersociety Convention, 29-31 May 1943, pp. 1-2, APA Coll., box I6.

24. "Recommendations of the Intersociety Constitutional Convention of Psychologists," *Psychological Bulletin* 40 (November 1943): 624.

25. *Proceedings of the Emergency Committee in Psychology*, 6-7 August 1943, Willard C. Olson Papers, AHAP, box M147.

26. "Recommendations," p. 626.

27. Ibid., pp. 626-45.

28. Edward E. Anderson, "A Note on the Proposed By-laws for a Reconstituted APA," *Psychological Bulletin* 41 (April 1944), 230-34.

29. Harriet E. O'Shea and Gilbert J. Rich to presidents, secretaries, and representatives to the Board of Affiliates of Affiliated Societies, n.d. [11 March 1944], APA Coll., box K4.

30. Alice I. Bryan to Harriet E. O'Shea, 18 April 1944, APA Coll., box K4.

31. Alice I. Bryan to C. M. Louttit, 20 May 1944, APA Coll., box K1.

32. Willard C. Olson, *Proceedings of the Fifty-Third Annual Meeting of the American Psychological Association*, in *Psychological Bulletin* 42 (December 1945): 706, 713.

33. Joy P. Guilford, "Some Lessons from Aviation Psychology," *American Psychologist* 3 (January 1948): 10.

7. APPLIED PSYCHOLOGY IN THE POSTWAR ERA

1. Moss Hart, *Winged Victory* (New York: Random House, 1943), Act 1, scene 4 pp. 42-45. Quotation is from pp. 43-44.

2. Ward Morehouse in the *New York Sun*, November 22, 1943, as reproduced in "Winged Victory," *New York Theatre Critics Reviews* 4 (22 November 1943): 216-19.

3. Leslie Halliwell, *The Filmgoer's Companion*, 4th ed., (New York: Hill and Wang, 1974), p. 624.

4. William Brinkley, "Valley Forge GIs Tell of Their Brainwashing Ordeal," *Life*, 25 May 1953, p. 108.

5. Loren Baritz, *The Servants of Power* (Middletown, Conn.: Wesleyan University Press, 1960), pp. 139-55.

6. William H. Whyte, *The Organization Man* (New York: Simon and Schuster, 1956), chs. 14, 15, and appendix.

7. J[oseph] W[olpe] and L[eo] J. R[eyna], editorial, *Journal of Behavior Therapy and Experimental Psychiatry* 1 (March 1970): 1.

8. Eleanor Criswell and Severin Peterson, "The Whole Soul Catalog," *Psychology Today*, April 1972, p. 58.

9. Norman D. Sundberg, Leona E. Tyler, and Julian R. Taplin, *Clinical Psychology: Expanding Horizons*, 2nd ed. (New York: Appleton-Century-Crofts, 1973), p. 532.

10. Jules Asher, "Psychonomy: Psychology: Astronomy: Astrology," *APA Monitor*, January 1975, pp. 1, 10.

11. Matthew W. Baird to Robert R. Sears, 26 March 1951, APA Coll., box H2.

CONCLUSION

1. P. 3.

2. Robert W. Hodge, Paul M. Siegel, and Peter H. Rossi, "Occupational Prestige in the United States," *American Journal of Sociology* 70 (November 1964): 290-91, table 1.

INDEX